Grammar Rules!

Tanya Gibb

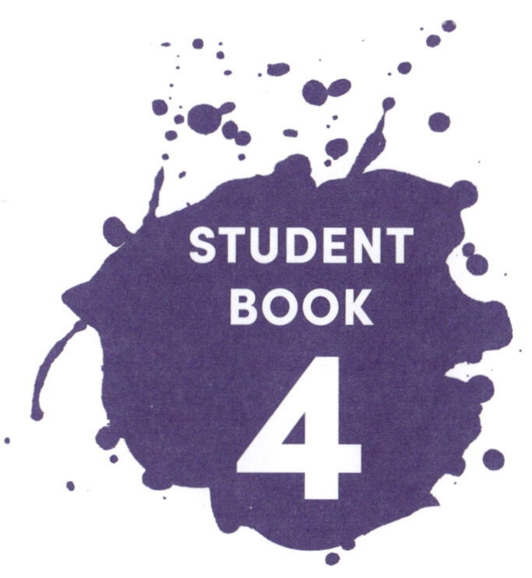

Australian Curriculum Edition

Name: ______________________________

Class: ______________________________

Grammar Rules! Student Book 4
Australian Curriculum Edition
ISBN: 978 0 6550 9252 0

Designer and typesetter: Trish Hayes
Illustrator: Stephen Michael King
Series editor: Marie James
Indigenous consultant: Al Fricker

Acknowledgement of Country
Matilda Education Australia acknowledges all Aboriginal and Torres Strait Islander Traditional Custodians of Country and recognises their continuing connection to land, sea, culture, and community. We pay our respects to Elders past and present.

This edition published in 2024 by **Matilda Education Australia**, an imprint of Meanwhile Education Pty
PO Box 118, Burwood, Victoria, Australia 3125
T: 1300 277 235
E: customersupport@matildaed.com.au
W: www.matildaeducation.com.au

First edition published in 2008 by Macmillan Science and Education Australia Pty Ltd

Publication data
Author: Tanya Gibb
Title: *Grammar Rules! Student Book 4 Australian Curriculum Edition*
ISBN: 978 0 6550 9252 0

A catalogue record for this book is available from the National Library of Australia

Printed in China by Central
Sep-23

Contents

NOTE TO TEACHERS AND PARENTS

Grammar Rules!

Grammar Rules! comprehensively addresses the interrelated strands of Language, Literature and Literacy in the **Australian Curriculum English V9**, 2022. The *Grammar Rules!* series supports students' development of knowledge, understanding and skills in reading, viewing, speaking, writing and creating texts.

The **Australian Curriculum English** recognises that learning in English is recursive and cumulative, so each book in the *Grammar Rules!* series is designed to build on concepts covered previously and for an expanding range of audiences and purposes.

Grammar Rules! provides a conceptually sound scope and sequence of context-based activities that support teaching and learning in English. Although the title for the series is *Grammar Rules!*, the series in not just about grammar. Each unit of work in the series begins at the level of the whole text by identifying purpose and audience for the model text, providing teaching opportunities to activate students' background knowledge of the topic or the text type, and then supporting students in reading comprehension. The texts provided can be used for discussion of text forms and features and sentence structures, as well as for vocabulary expansion. The texts can also be used as models for students to use when creating their own written, spoken or multimodal texts. The texts included in *Grammar Rules!* cover a variety of informative, imaginative and persuasive texts and hybrid texts that use elements of different types of texts.

Grammar Rules! also teaches the conventions of punctuation and some aspects of spelling, such as prefixes, suffixes, apostrophes and homophones, and literary elements, such as onomatopoeia, simile and idiom, as well as character, setting and plot in narratives. *Grammar Rules!* comprehensively supports the aim of the **Australian Curriculum English V9** to 'help students learn to analyse, understand, communicate and build relationships with others and the world around them. It helps create confident communicators, imaginative and critical thinkers, and informed citizens.'

Student Book 4

UNITS OF WORK

Student Book 4 contains 35 weekly units of work presented in a conceptually sound scope and sequence. The intention is for students to work through the units in the sequence in which they are presented. See the **Scope and Sequence Chart** on pages 6–7 for more information. There are regular Revision Units that can be used for consolidation or assessment purposes.

The sample texts in *Student Book 4* are not tied to any particular content across other curriculum areas but are generally based on the theme of water. This allows teachers and students to focus on the way language is structured in the different types of texts according to purpose and audience. Students can then use this knowledge to critically evaluate, respond to and create texts in other learning areas.

ICONS

Encourages students to create texts of their own to demonstrate their understanding of the text structures and features taught in the unit. These activities focus on written language; however, many also provide opportunities for using spoken language to engage with others, make presentations and develop skills in using ICT.

Highlights useful grammatical rules and concepts. The rule is always introduced the first time students need it to complete an activity.

Tells students that a special hint is provided for an activity. It might be a tip about language features or a reminder to look at a rule in a previous unit.

GRAMMAR RULES! GLOSSARY

A valuable glossary is provided at the end of *Student Book 4*. Teachers and students can use this as a reference for terminology and rules introduced in *Student Book 4*. Page references are also given for the point in the book where the rule or tip was first introduced so that students can go back to that unit if they need more information or further revision of the concept.

Grammar Rules! Student Book 4 (ISBN 9780655092520) © Tanya Gibb

Pull-Out Writing Log

At the centre of *Student Book 4* is a practical pull-out Writing Log so that students can keep track of the texts they have created or attempted to create. The Writing Log also includes a handy reminder of the writing process, as well as a checklist of types of texts for students to try.

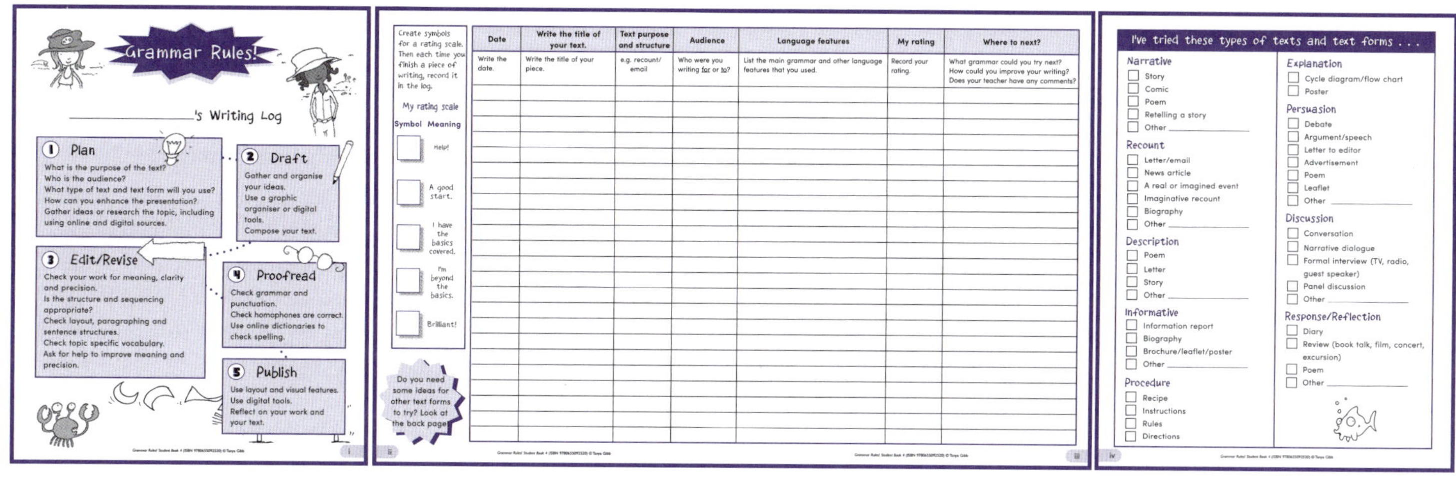

Grammar Rules!

_______________'s Writing Log

1 Plan
What is the purpose of the text?
Who is the audience?
What type of text and text form will you use?
How can you enhance the presentation?
Gather ideas or research the topic, including using online and digital sources.

2 Draft
Gather and organise your ideas.
Use a graphic organiser or digital tools.
Compose your text.

3 Edit/Revise
Check your work for meaning, clarity and precision.
Is the structure and sequencing appropriate?
Check layout, paragraphing and sentence structures.
Check topic specific vocabulary.
Ask for help to improve meaning and precision.

4 Proofread
Check grammar and punctuation.
Check homophones are correct.
Use online dictionaries to check spelling.

5 Publish
Use layout and visual features.
Use digital tools.
Reflect on your work and your text.

Create symbols for a rating scale. Then each time you finish a piece of writing, record it in the log.

My rating scale

Symbol	Meaning
	Help!
	A good start.
	I have the basics covered.
	I'm beyond the basics.
	Brilliant!

Do you need some ideas for other text forms to try? Look at the back page.

Date	Write the title of your text.	Text purpose and structure	Audience	Language features	My rating	Where to next?
Write the date.	Write the title of your piece.	e.g. recount/email	Who were you writing for or to?	List the main grammar and other language features that you used.	Record your rating.	What grammar could you try next? How could you improve your writing? Does your teacher have any comments?

I've tried these types of texts and text forms . . .

Narrative: Story; Comic; Poem; Retelling a story; Other ______

Recount: Letter/email; News article; A real or imagined event; Imaginative recount; Biography; Other ______

Description: Poem; Letter; Story; Other ______

Informative: Information report; Biography; Brochure/leaflet/poster; Other ______

Procedure: Recipe; Instructions; Rules; Directions

Explanation: Cycle diagram/flow chart; Poster

Persuasion: Debate; Argument/speech; Letter to editor; Advertisement; Poem; Leaflet; Other ______

Discussion: Conversation; Narrative dialogue; Formal interview (TV, radio, guest speaker); Panel discussion; Other ______

Response/Reflection: Diary; Review (book talk, film, concert, excursion); Poem; Other ______

Unit At A Glance

Unit tag
States the main grammar focus

Type of text
Highlights the type of text and purpose of the sample text

Rule!
Introduces students to a new concept

Text sample
Provides a context for learning about language

Sequenced activities
Activities focus on reading comprehension, text features and structures, vocabulary, grammar or punctuation

Tip!
Reminds or gives a special hint

Try it yourself!
Gives students opportunities to apply their knowledge and skills to create their own texts. Students can engage in planning, drafting and editing their texts and using different modes and media to enhance presentation of their texts.

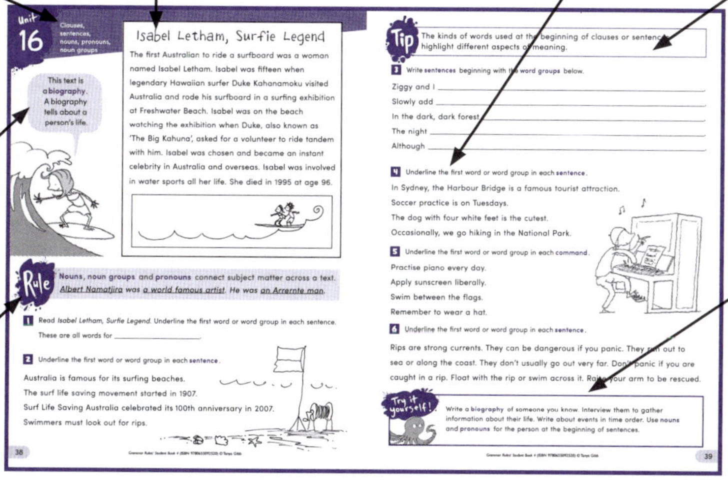

Grammar Rules! Teacher Resource Book 3–6

Full teacher support for *Student Book 4* is provided by *Grammar Rules! Teacher Resource Book 3–6*. Here you will find valuable background information about teaching English along with practical resources, such as:

- strategies for teaching text structures and features
- literacy games and activities
- assessment strategies
- grammar and punctuation wall charts
- teaching tips for every unit in *Student Book 4*
- answers for every unit in *Student Book 4*.

Scope and Sequence

This scope and sequence chart is based on the requirements of the Australian Curriculum English.

Unit	Unit name Type of text	Purpose of text	Clauses, sentences, conjunctions, connectives	Nouns, noun groups, pronouns, adjectives	Verbs and verb groups	Adverbs, adverbials, prepositional phrases	Elements of language
1	**Dear Dad** Recount – email	to retell events to respond		proper and common nouns	doing (action) and saying verbs, past tense		summarising
2	**Shark** Narrative – orientation	to entertain	clauses, conjunctions, sentences		thinking verbs		
3	**Auslan** Definition Response	to inform to respond	quoted and reported speech	personal pronouns	saying verbs		opinions
4	**Australia's Mightiest River System** Information report	to inform	sentences, statements, clauses	noun groups, articles, adjectives	relating verbs		
5	**Kakadu Seasons** Poem	to entertain to describe		noun groups, adjectives			poetic language, imagery, synonyms antonyms, affixes
6	REVISION						
7	**How to Save Water** Instructions	to instruct	commands		doing (action) verbs	prepositional phrases	apostrophes for contractions, commas
8	**Our Dam** Recount	to inform to reflect		singular, plural and collective nouns			homophones
9	**Dear Mum** Recount – email	to inform to respond		possessive pronouns, possessive adjectives			chronological order, apostrophes for possession, familiar audience
10	**Sun Safety** Instructions	to inform to instruct	compound sentences, conjunctions, clauses	noun groups	tense, verbs		
11	**The Driest Place on Earth** Information report	to inform	statements, questions, clauses, conjunctions				technical terminology, unfamiliar audience
12	REVISION						
13	**Frog Potion** Recipe/Instructions	to entertain	commands		doing (action) verbs	prepositional phrases	numbered (logical) order
14	**How to Work in a Group** Instructions	to instruct to inform	commands		doing (action) verbs	adverbs	
15	**Directions to the Olympic Pool** Directions	to instruct to inform	commands	proper nouns	doing (action) verbs		numbered (logical) order
16	**Isabel Letham, Surfie Legend** Biography	to inform	clauses, sentences	nouns, pronouns, noun groups	verbs	phrases	sentence beginnings
17	**Recycled Water** Explanation	to inform to explain			verbs, verb groups, tense		flow diagrams
18	REVISION						

Unit	Unit name Type of text	Purpose of text	Clauses, sentences, conjunctions, connectives	Nouns, noun groups, pronouns, adjectives	Verbs and verb groups	Adverbs, adverbials, prepositional phrases	Elements of language
19	**Sewerage Wanted** News report	to inform to entertain	quoted and reported speech				emotive words, main idea, comic strip, speech balloons, dialogue
20	**We Tank You** Advertisement	to persuade		personal pronouns, possessive adjectives	doing (action) verbs		emotive words, synonyms
21	**Kati Thanda-Lake Eyre** Information report	to inform to describe	complex sentences, conjunctions	comparative and superlative adjectives, adjectival clauses			simile
22	**The BFG** Book talk	to respond to persuade	conjunctions	adjectives			word play – neologism, spoonerism, pun
23	**Say NO to Plastic!** A call to action	to persuade	dependent and independent clauses, conjunctions	personal pronouns	verbs		emotive language, opinions, main idea, commas
24	REVISION						
25	**Cane Toads** Formal interview/ Talk show format	to entertain to inform to influence		noun groups that classify			subjective/objective language, inclusive language
26	**Lucky to be Alive!** News report	to inform	sentences	noun groups	verb groups, modal verbs	modal adverbs	emotive verbs
27	**Missing from History** Poem	to persuade to reflect			noun-verb agreement		subjective/objective language, reference sources
28	**Too Cruel!** Argument Formal speech	to argue a point of view	connectives, conjunctions				emotive language, formal language, opinions
29	**Tsunami** Information report	to inform	subordinating conjunctions		verb groups, suffixes		
30	REVISION						
31	**Vote Against School Swimming** Speech/Argument	to persuade to argue a point of view	connectives	pronouns	modal verbs	modal adverbs	main idea, opinions, summarising
32	**First Nations Words** Glossary	to inform	dependent and independent clauses	pronouns		adverbial clauses	glossary
33	**Floods and Wildlife** Leaflet/Brochure	to inform	clauses	determiners, articles			emotive words, synonyms
34	**The Quest to Save Allura** Narrative	to entertain		determiners		adverbs, prepositional phrases	flashback, first- and third-person narrator, tension
35	REVISION						

Unit 1

Common and proper nouns, verbs

Dear Dad

Mum and Dave drove us to Sandy Beach on Saturday. As soon as we got there, I slathered on my sunscreen and went for a swim. After a while, the waves started to get really rough so I helped Bella build a sandcastle. When it started to get cold, Mum announced it was time to leave. We shook off all the sand and got in the car and headed home. On the way home, we stopped for ice creams. Mine was strawberry-flavoured. It was really yummy!

See you in the school holidays.

Love, Elijah

This text is a **personal recount** for a **familiar audience**. Events are recounted in time order.

1 Read *Dear Dad*. Summarise the events in a time sequence. Number the events.

Rule

Nouns name people, places, animals and things, including ideas.

friends *river* *classroom* *turtles* *happiness* *cruelty*

Proper nouns begin with a capital letter.

Stephen *Australia* *Hector's dolphin* *Disability Services Australia*

2 Circle the **proper nouns** in *Dear Dad*.

3 Rewrite the sentences with correct punctuation.

did jasmine and daniel have a holiday in darwin, garramilla

I hope maria can come to my house on wednesday

my birthday is in march and your birthday is in may

Verbs tell what's happening in clauses. **Doing verbs** tell the actions. The form of the verb can tell you if the action happened in the past. This is called **past tense**.

4 Underline the **past tense doing verbs**.

I jumped over the fence.

Dad cooked dinner.

Mum fixed my bike.

He swam slowly.

She walked swiftly.

5 Write the **past tense** forms for each **doing verb**. Hint! You'll find them all in *Dear Dad*.

slather ____________

start ____________

help ____________

shake ____________

stop ____________

6 Change the form of the **doing verb** in brackets so that the event happened in the past.

I (ride) ____________ a bike to school.

We (eat) ____________ apples for morning tea.

Mum (buys) ____________ bananas at the fruit market.

Grandpa (bounces) ____________ the basketball.

Rule

Saying verbs tell you that something has been said.

7 Write the **saying verb** in *Dear Dad*.

____

8 Write a **saying verb** on each line.

Mum ____________ , 'Hurry up, we're late for school!'

'I want one too!' ____________ my little brother.

'Let's get out of here,' ____________ Jessie.

'Where are we?' ____________ Lou.

'We'd better be quiet,' ____________ Manish.

Try it yourself!

Write your own **recount** about something that happened to you last weekend. Use **nouns** for people, places and things. Remember to use the **past tense** forms of the **verbs**.

Unit 2 Thinking verbs, clauses, conjunctions

This text is the **orientation** for a **narrative**. It uses **thinking verbs** for the main character's thoughts and feelings.

Shark

Jo loved sharks. She thought they were amazing animals.

Jo was excited today because her uncle had finally agreed to let her go on his boat during a shark-tagging expedition. Her uncle was a shark biologist. His team was tagging white sharks with acoustic tags. The tags allow researchers to see how far sharks travel over a year and where they travel to.

Jo had been nagging for months to be allowed on an expedition, but her uncle had always claimed that it was too dangerous for a ten-year-old. She wondered what the day would bring.

Rule

Thinking verbs represent mental activities by using words such as *loved*, *believed*, *disliked* and *worried*. You can't see these activities taking place.

1 Read *Shark*. Circle the **thinking verbs** in the first paragraph.

2 What might Jo be hoping *the day would bring*?

____

What do you think could happen in the story?

____

3 Write **thinking verbs** from the box to complete each sentence.

hoped
respected
felt
worried
feared

Jo's uncle ____________ sharks.

Jo's uncle ____________ about Jo's safety.

Jo ____________ they'd tag a shark.

Jo ____________ proud that her uncle had an important job.

Jo ____________ for the survival of sharks.

Grammar Rules! Student Book 4 (ISBN 9780655092520) © Tanya Gibb

A **clause** is a unit of meaning that must include a **verb**.
A **simple sentence** is one clause. **Conjunctions** join clauses.

Amir read every night. He finished the book in a week.

Amir read every night and he finished the book in a week.

4 Use **conjunctions** *and, but, so, or* to join the sentences. Write the new sentences on the lines.

I like pumpkin. I don't like Brussels sprouts.

___

It rained all day. We weren't allowed outside.

___

We might get there by 10 am. We might get there after 10 am.

___

I studied hard. I won the spelling contest.

___

5 Add a **clause** to complete each sentence.

Jo likes sharks because ___

Jo behaved well on the trip so ___

They caught a bull shark but ___

The weather was fine but ___

Jo's uncle decided to take Jo because ___

Jo took a photo so ___

Write an orientation for a story. Use **thinking verbs** to represent the way the characters think and feel. Or, write what might happen next in *Shark*. Use thinking verbs to tell readers how Jo feels about events.

Unit 3

Quoted speech, reported speech

These texts on the topic of Auslan have different **purposes**. All three are **informative** but Texts 2 and 3 also present **opinions**.

Auslan

Text 1: Auslan is the visual language of the Australian deaf community. It uses two-handed signs and a two-handed alphabet.

Text 2: Sam's father says that Sam is learning Auslan so that he can communicate better with his best friend, Arthur. Sam's father told Sam that he is proud of him.

Text 3: 'I'm really happy to be learning Auslan,' said Sam. 'I've been learning it for over a year now and I'm pretty good at it. It's fun and Arthur is my best friend, so I want to use his language. He's used Auslan since birth so he's brilliant. He's also a better swimmer than me!'

Rule

Quoted speech (direct speech) is the speech someone said. It is written inside **quotation marks**. These can be single '...' or double "...". A comma usually separates the speech from the rest of the sentence.

'Auslan is a clever language,' said Maya.

Reported speech (indirect speech) is speech that is not directly quoted.

Maya said that Auslan is a clever language.

1. Read *Auslan*. Circle the **saying verbs**. Underline the **quoted speech**.

2. Which text/s in *Auslan* use **reported speech**? ______________________

3. Rewrite each sentence. Use punctuation marks.

you are a good friend said arthur

____

where did rowan go asked rachel

____

sam told everyone that he and arthur swim every wednesday and saturday

____

Grammar Rules! Student Book 4 (ISBN 9780655092520) © Tanya Gibb

Rule

A **pronoun** is a word that replaces a noun. **Personal pronouns** link a person or thing across a text.

I me we us you he she it her him they them

Arthur enjoys swimming. He is a member of the Southport Dolphins Swim Club.

4 Write a **personal pronoun** on each line.

Auslan is a visual language. __________ uses two-handed signing.

Bill said, 'Auslan is good for Sam's brain. __________ is doing well to learn __________.'

Arthur and Sam are both in 4H. __________ also belong to the same swim club.

'Arthur and I love swimming,' said Sam. '__________ swim twice a week.'

5 Rewrite each sentence as **quoted speech**.

Sam said that his Auslan teacher's name is Ms Petrović.

____

Ms Petrović said that learning Auslan improves people's memory.

____

The principal announced that the school had received a sustainability award.

____

Tip

I and *me* can be tricky when you are talking about yourself and someone else. To choose the correct **personal pronoun** follow this pattern:

I went to the shop. → *Ben and I went to the shop.*

Mum bought me a cake. → *Mum bought Ben and me cakes.*

6 Join the following sentences correctly using either *me* or *I*.

Jai ate an apple. I ate an apple.	Jai and ______ ate apples.
Dad helped me. Dad helped Debbie.	Dad helped Debbie and ______.

Try it yourself!

Write a recount about something you have done. Use **personal pronouns**. Include **quoted speech** and/or **reported speech**.

Unit 4

Relating verbs, noun groups

This **information report** uses **relating verbs** and **noun groups** to describe a river system.

Australia's Mightiest River System

Australia's longest river is the Murray. It is 2508 kilometres long. It travels through New South Wales and South Australia.

Australia's longest river system is the Murray-Darling, which starts in Queensland as the Darling River and ends in South Australia, where the Murray River flows into the sea. The Murray-Darling system is 3370 kilometres long.

The Murray-Darling river system supports sixteen internationally important wetlands and the wildlife that needs them to survive. The river system is at risk from climate change, pollution, dams and introduced species of fish and plants.

Rule

Relating verbs show relationships, such as being and having. You cannot see any action taking place.

is *belongs* *equals* *was* *had* *are* *has*

1 Read *Australia's Mightiest River System*. Then circle the **relating verbs** in the following statements.

The river is 3370 kilometres long.

The river has a number of problems.

The river is polluted.

The river belongs to a system of waterways.

2 Choose a **relating verb** from the box to complete each sentence.

is	belongs	equals	was	had	are

Two plus two __________ four.

My favourite food __________ lasagne but now I prefer spaghetti.

It __________ lunchtime.

You __________ my best friend.

The lunch box __________ to Bintang.

Jodie __________ a photo of a bunyip.

Grammar Rules! Student Book 4 (ISBN 9780655092520) © Tanya Gibb

A **sentence** consists of one or more clauses. Every **clause** must have a **verb**. A sentence ends in a full stop, question mark or exclamation mark.

3 Circle the **verbs** in the **sentences** below.

The WWF conducts surveys.

Rivers are powerful.

The crocodile had a delicious lunch.

The canoe crashed over the waterfall.

I thought the pirate was ugly.

4 Unjumble these words to write **sentences** from *Australia's Mightiest River System*. Use correct punctuation.

longest river the murray is australia's ____________________

is 3370 long kilometres it ____________________

travels through it new south wales and south australia

____

A **noun group** is a group of words built around a noun to tell more about the noun. A noun group can include **articles** (*a, an, the*), **adjectives** that describe or tell number and other **nouns** used to classify.

an incredible river system *many swooping kingfishers*

the wetland environment

5 Circle the **noun groups**.

The Murray-Darling Basin supports important wetlands.

The lower River Murray is Ngarrindjeri Country.

Many waterbirds rely on the wetlands.

The Basin has formed over hundreds of millions of years.

The Basin's rivers meander across giant flood plains.

Use the internet. Do some research on a place of your choice in Australia. Create an **information report**. Add images and create a short slide show to present the information to the class.

Poetic language, noun groups, synonyms, antonyms

This **poem** has two stanzas. Each stanza is a **cinquain**. The poem uses **noun groups** to build descriptions.

Kakadu Seasons

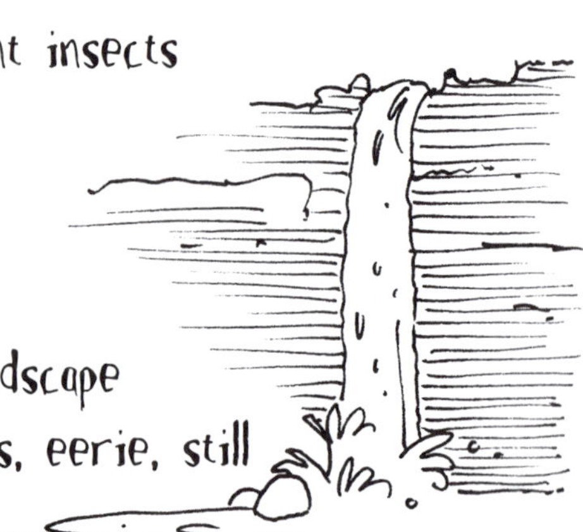

Wetlands
Soaked air
Vibrant, colourful flowers
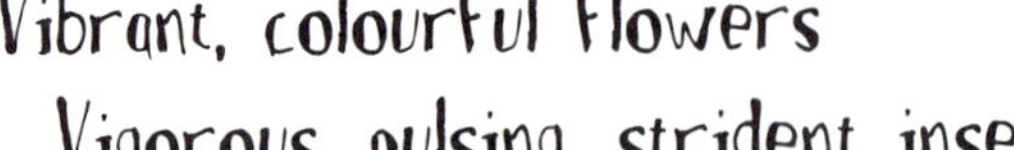
Vigorous, pulsing, strident insects
Profusion.

Drylands
Heated air
Rocky, parched landscape
Expectant, breathless, eerie, still
Waiting.

Rule Poetic language, including using adjectives, can help to bring subject matter to life and engage readers and listeners emotionally.

1 Read *Kakadu Seasons*. Write **adjectives** from the poem that describe these **nouns**.

insects ____________________

flowers ____________________

landscape ____________________

air ____________________

2 Underline the **descriptive adjectives** in these **noun groups**.

colourful grasshoppers

hungry dangerous crocodiles

timid little quolls

large grey cranes

Rule **Synonyns** are words with similar meanings: (*vivid-bright*). **Antonyms** are words with opposite meanings: (*bright-dull*). Some antonyms are formed using a **suffix** (*careful-careless*) or a **prefix** (*do-undo*).

3 Write a **synonym** for each word below as it is used in *Kakadu Seasons*.

parched ____________ vibrant ____________

pulsing ____________ expectant ____________

4 Write five **synonyms** for *strident*. Use a dictionary.

__________ __________ __________ __________ __________

Grammar Rules! Student Book 4 (ISBN 9780655092520) © Tanya Gibb

5 Write **antonyms** for these words from *Kakadu Seasons*.

parched ________________ vibrant ________________

pulsing ________________ strident ________________

6 Read *Kakadu Seasons* again.

If you stood in the wetlands, how would you feel?

____

If you stood in the drylands, how would you feel?

____

Which senses does *Kakadu Seasons* appeal to? Circle the ones that apply.

hearing taste smell touch sight

7 Change the **adjectives** to give each description a different meaning.

The <u>handsome young</u> man stepped out of his <u>battered old car</u>.

____

The <u>fit older</u> lady ate her <u>small healthy</u> meal.

____

The <u>energetic little</u> dog waited for her <u>busy</u> owner.

____

8 Write your own **descriptive adjectives**.

______________ Suraya tripped over the ______________ dog.

______________ ______________ Desmond walked quietly along the ______________ street.

______________ Pete drove too fast on the ______________ road.

I couldn't wait to read my ______________ ______________ book.

Kakadu Seasons is made up of two cinquains. A cinquain is a poem with five lines. The structure is one word, two words, three words, four words, one word. Write your own cinquain. Use **adjectives** to appeal to the senses.

Unit 6

Revision

1 Underline the **relating verbs.**

Many wetland species are endangered.

The biggest recorded Murray cod was 1.8m.

The brown trout is an introduced species.

The carp has become an environmental problem.

2 Underline the **doing verbs.**

I stepped on a thumbtack.

Dad grated the carrots for the salad.

Mum mowed the lawn.

Katy cooked spaghetti.

Melek picked flowers.

3 Change the form of the **doing verbs** in the sentences so that the events happened in the **past.**

The sheep (hop) ________________ over the log.

We (eat) ________________ Anzac biscuits.

Vince (buys) ________________ vegetables at the market.

Nonna (walks) ________________ to the shop.

4 Write a **saying verb** on each line.

Mum ________________, 'Time for bed.'

'I'll share with you,' ________________ my little brother.

'Go away!' ________________ Jessie.

'Where did you put my book?' ________________ Tam.

Dad ________________, 'Somebody needs to clean the mouse cage.'

5 Rewrite each sentence using correct punctuation.

aunty said I donate to a charity called rainforest alliance

____

I told andre to come after school on friday

____

my birthday is in september and emily's birthday is in october

____

Grammar Rules! Student Book 4 (ISBN 9780655092520) © Tanya Gibb

6 Circle the **thinking verbs**.

I believe she is telling the truth.

I think my cat is the cutest.

The coach worried about the game.

7 Rewrite each sentence below as **reported speech**.

'The shark is an apex predator,' said Mr Yang.

____

'What's an apex predator?' asked Remy.

____

8 Join these sentences using a **conjunction** from the box. Write the new sentence on the line.

so	but	because

I walked to the shop. I caught a bus home.

____

It was a beautiful sunny day. We went on a picnic.

____

I was allowed to watch television. I had finished all my homework.

____

9 Circle all the **noun groups**.

The great ancestral cod, Ponde, was chased by a great hunter, Ngurunderi.

The cod thrashed about and swung its powerful tail, and formed the bends and billabongs of the Murray River.

10 Rewrite the paragraph below by replacing the underlined words with **personal pronouns**.

My family and I play tennis. <u>My family and I</u> play each Saturday. The exercise keeps <u>my family and me</u> fit.

____

____

11 Write three **synonyms** for *noisy*. __________ __________ __________

Unit 7

Commands, prepositional phrases, commas, contractions

This text includes **instructions**. The text title states the goal. The text begins with an introduction. It uses subheadings and dot points.

HOW TO SAVE WATER

Saving water is important, even in times of flood, because saving water saves the energy it takes to get water into homes and heat it.

Indoors

- Take shorter showers (under 4 minutes).
- Turn off the tap when brushing your teeth.
- Rinse dishes in a half-full sink and not under running water.

Outdoors

- Use a trigger hose, bucket or watering can.
- Wash the car on the lawn.
- Use a broom on paving and not a hose.
- Plant water-efficient native trees and plants.
- Collect your shower water in a bucket (while waiting for it to heat) and use it on your plants.
- Install a rainwater tank.

1 Read *How to Save Water*. Why should you try to use less water?

Commands tell someone to do something. Commands usually begin with a **verb**. *Don't tread on the flowers.* *Think about it.*
Instructions use commands to help people achieve a goal.

2 In *How to Save Water*, circle ten **doing verbs** that begin the **commands**.

3 In *How to Save Water*, tick the dot points that you could try in your home.

Use a comma to separate items in a list. *Bring a bucket, soap and gloves.*

4 Copy the sentence in *How to Save Water* that uses a comma in a list.

Grammar Rules! Student Book 4 (ISBN 9780655092520) © Tanya Gibb

A **prepositional phrase** can tell time, place or manner (*when, where, how*). It begins with a preposition (e.g. *for, in, on, from, for, by, with, to*) and includes a **noun** or **pronoun**.

for an hour   *in the oven*   *over the moon*   *with us*   *with a wooden spoon*

5 Underline five **prepositional phrases** in *How to Save Water.*

6 Add a **prepositional phrase** of your own to complete the sentences.

Let's go to the park ______________________________.

Put the remote ______________________________.

The contest took place ______________________________.

The novel was written ______________________________.

A **contraction** is a word made by combining two or more words and leaving letters out. **Apostrophes** are used to mark the place of the missing letters.   *do not – don't*   *it is – it's*   *I am – I'm*

7 Draw a line to link the words in the top row to their **contractions** underneath.

will not   you will   was not   can not   it is   they are   I will   must not   he is   were not

I'll   won't   mustn't   he's   it's   weren't   can't   they're   you'll   wasn't

8 Write a **contraction** from the box on each line. Use a capital letter if the contraction begins a sentence.

it's shouldn't don't it's they're that'll

Save water. ______________ waste water.

Turn the tap off. ______________ wasteful to leave the water running.

Wash the car on the lawn. ______________ save watering the lawn.

Sweep the paving. You ______________ hose it.

Native plants are best. ______________ usually more water efficient.

Don't waste water. ______________ precious.

Write a set of **instructions** for how to do something. It could be how to find a buried treasure, how to play a game or how to help the environment. Use **commands**. Publish and share your work.

Unit **8** Singular, plural and collective nouns, homophones

Our Dam

Last June, my parents borrowed a neighbour's backhoe. They used it to dig a second dam so our herd of cows would have more water. It took a whole weekend to dig a hole that was deep enough and wide enough, and they had just finished when the rain came. After a few weeks of wet weather, the dam was full and a flock of ducks had moved in.

We haven't had any rain since then. My mum has used the water in that dam to irrigate our vegetables for the past eight months, but the water is nearly all gone now. We are all hoping for rain.

1 Read *Our Dam*. Write **nouns** from *Our Dam* that these **adjectives** could describe.

deep, wide ____________________

noisy ____________________

heavy, soaking ____________________

hard-working ____________________

favourite, fresh ____________________

generous, helpful ____________________

wet, flooding ____________________

hopeful ____________________

2 Circle *it* and *It* in *Our Dam*. Write two things that the **pronouns** replace.

____

Homophones are words that sound the same but are spelled differently and have different meanings.

plane/plain *flower/flour* *Use plain flour in the cake.*

3 Write five **homophones** used in *Our Dam*. Write their homophone pairs.

____

____

Grammar Rules! Student Book 4 (ISBN 9780655092520) © Tanya Gibb

4 Use **homophones** *their, there* or *they're* in the sentences below.

We have good neighbours. We borrowed __________ lawnmower last week.

This morning, our neighbours asked Dad to return the lawnmower to __________ garage, but Dad said he had already left it __________. __________ going to be annoyed if __________ lawnmower is missing.

Rule

A **noun** can be **singular** or **plural**.
A noun can be made plural by:

- adding *–s* or *–es* on the end *parent parents peach peaches*
  If the base word ends in *y*, change *y* to *i* to add *-es*. *berry-berries*
- changing the spelling in another way *foot feet child children*

Some nouns don't change at all from singular to plural. *fish sheep*

5 Write the **plural** for each **singular noun**. Use a dictionary to check spelling.

half __________ kangaroo __________ radius __________

child __________ woman __________ baby __________

Rule

Collective nouns are names for groups of things. Collective nouns are singular. *The class is going to the library.*

6 Write two **collective nouns** in *Our Dam*.

__________ __________

7 Choose a **collective noun** from the box for each group.

pod	string	bouquet	team	fleet	pride

a __________ of whales

a __________ of footballers

a __________ of pearls

a __________ of lions

a __________ of ships

a __________ of flowers

Try it yourself!

Use a dictionary to find some **plural** and **singular nouns**. Find ten for each category: ends in *–s*, ends in *–es*, other spelling change, no spelling change. Compare your lists with a partner's lists.

Unit 9 Apostrophes for possession, possessive adjectives and pronouns

This text is **informative**. It retells events in a time sequence and includes a personal response. It is written for a **familiar, informal audience**.

Hello from the farm

Dear Mum,

I'm having a great time at Nan and Pop's farm. Last month, Lilly had a litter. Pop kept one of the puppies. Her name is Lulu. Yesterday I did some chores. First I cleaned out the chicken coop. The chickens were friendly, but their coop was smelly. I also cleaned the dogs' kennel. The dogs got excited when I went near their kennel because they thought I was going to give them their dinner. Pop's chores are much harder than mine. Tomorrow he will need to fix some fences.

There's still no water in the dam.

Love,
Skye

Rule

Possessive pronouns show ownership.

his *hers* *theirs* *yours* *mine* *ours*

The hat is <u>his</u>. *The farm is <u>theirs</u>.* *The book is <u>mine</u>.*

1 Complete each sentence with a **possessive pronoun** from the box.

his	hers	theirs	yours	mine	ours

Adam says that the book is ____________.

They told me that car was ____________.

Give that back to Shelly, it's ____________!

Take the prize. You won it, it's ____________.

It's my job to feed the fish, because they are ____________.

That house is ____________!

yours
mine
ours

2 Read *Dear Mum*. Circle the **possessive pronoun**. Hint! There is only one.

Grammar Rules! Student Book 4 (ISBN 9780655092520) © Tanya Gibb

Noun groups can include possessive adjectives to show possession.
<u>Our</u> old dog *his* *her* *their* *your* *my* *our* *its*

3 In *Dear Mum*, underline the **possessive adjectives** that show ownership. Hint! There are four.

4 Use a **possessive adjective** from the box to complete each sentence. If the pronoun begins a sentence, use a capital letter.

their	his	her	its

__________ boots are dirty. (Pop's boots)

I like __________ name. (Lulu's name)

__________ farm is fun. (Nan and Pop's farm)

I gave the cow __________ water. (the cow's water)

An **apostrophe** can show ownership. An apostrophe with a noun shows that something belongs to that noun.

singular noun	add *'s*	*Jim's dog*
plural noun ending in *s*	add *'*	*the ducks' pond*
plural noun not ending in *s*	add *'s*	*the children's cubbyhouse*

5 Rewrite each sentence using an **apostrophe**.

That is the coop belonging to the chickens. = That is the chickens' coop.

Those are the shoes belonging to the twins. = __________

Where is the dog that belongs to Amiri? = __________

The presents belonging to the children are here! = __________

That is the desk belonging to the teacher. = __________

Those are the yachts belonging to the sailors. = __________

Draw a storyboard for the events listed in Skye's email. Label each image in the storyboard with words to show the time. For example, *Last month*, *Yesterday*, *First* and so on. Share and compare your storyboard with others in your class.

Unit 10 Noun groups, verb tense

This text provides **instructions** written as commands. The **verbs** are in **present tense** because they tell what you should always do.

Sun Safety

- Slip on a dark-coloured, long-sleeved shirt.
- Slop on some SPF 30+ sunscreen.
- Slap on a wide-brimmed legionnaire or bucket-style sunhat.
- Slide on some Cancer Council Australia recommended sunglasses.
- Seek out some shade and avoid the sun between 10 am and 3 pm.

1 Read *Sun Safety*. Find six **doing verbs**. Write them on the line.

____

2 Read *Sun Safety*. Underline the **noun groups**.

An **independent clause** makes sense on its own. It doesn't depend on another clause to make sense. Two independent clauses joined by a **conjunction** (*and, so, but*) form a **compound sentence**.

3 Circle the **compound sentence** in *Sun Safety*.

4 Add a **conjunction** (*and, so, but*) to join each pair of sentences and form **compound sentences**.

I did not reapply my sunscreen. I got sunburnt.

____

I did not wear a hat. My face got sunburnt.

____

I wore a hat and sunscreen. I still got sunburnt.

____

I'll wear my hat. I'll reapply sunscreen every two hours.

____

Grammar Rules! Student Book 4 (ISBN 9780655092520)

5 Rewrite the sentences with **quoted speech** as **reported speech**.

'I remembered to take my hat,' said Connor.

____

'Does your hat have a wide brim?' asked Yasmin.

____

Tip Remember the rule on page 12.

Rule **Verbs** can show whether an action happened in the past, is happening now, happens always or has not yet happened. This is called the **tense**.

past tense	*she went*	
present tense	*she is going*	*she goes*
future tense	*she will go*	

tick toc

6 Change the **verb** form so that the events happened in the **past**. Write the new sentence.

Present timeless tense	**Past tense**
She <u>eats</u> salad for lunch.	______________________
Tibby <u>jumps</u> on the bed.	______________________
Gran <u>drives</u> to work.	______________________
Dad <u>listens</u> to music.	______________________
My dog <u>slips</u> on tiles.	______________________

7 Change the **verbs** to **past tense**. Then use the past tense verbs to complete the sentences.

slip __________ slop __________ go __________

slap __________ slide __________

When I __________ to the beach, I __________ on a shirt, __________ on some sunscreen and __________ on a hat. I also __________ on some sunglasses.

Try it yourself! Write a set of **instructions** for safety in your home or school. You can make the instructions serious or funny. Ask classmates if your instructions are easy to follow. Edit your instructions before publishing and displaying them.

Unit 11

Questions and statements, clauses, conjunctions

This **information report** makes factual statements. It includes **technical terms**. It was written for an **unfamiliar audience**.

The Driest Place on Earth

Antarctica is approximately twice the size of Australia. Seventy per cent of the world's fresh water is frozen in Antarctica. Even though it holds more water than all the other continents combined, Antarctica is the driest continent on earth. It is called a frozen desert. Antarctica is also the windiest continent on earth, with hurricane-force winds reaching up to 250 kilometres per hour. The coldest temperature ever recorded, –89.6 °C, also belongs to Antarctica. After Antarctica, Australia is the next driest continent on earth.

Rule

A **statement** gives information or an opinion. It ends in a full stop.

Penguins live in Antartica. *Penguins are cute.*

A **question** asks for information or an opinion. It ends in a question mark. A question can be open or closed. Open questions ask for more detailed answers. *What is the time?* *What do you think of the story so far?*

1 Read *The Driest Place on Earth*. Find and write four statements from the text on the 'Answer' lines below. Write a Question for each answer.

Question: How big is Antarctica compared to Australia?

Answer: Antarctica is approximately twice the size of Australia.

Question: ______________________________

Answer: ______________________________

Question: ______________________________

Answer: ______________________________

Question: ______________________________

Answer: ______________________________

2 **Relating verbs** are common in **information reports**.
Circle the relating verbs in *The Driest Place on Earth*. How many did you find? ☐

Grammar Rules! Student Book 4 (ISBN 9780655092520) © Tanya Gibb

3 Write **statement** or **question** after each sentence. Then finish each sentence with the correct punctuation marker.

When will we eat dinner ______________ Where are my keys ______________

We'll eat dinner at 6 pm ______________ Did you phone Uncle Van ______________

Why did the two children disagree ______________

4 Write an open **question** beginning with each word. Remember to use a question mark at the end.

Who ____

What ____

When ____

Where ____

Why ____

How ____

Rule

A **dependent clause** depends on another clause to fully make sense. **Conjunctions** that join dependent clauses to an **independent clause** in a complex sentence include *when, until, although, if, since, because, after.*

5 Choose a **conjunction** from the box to join each pair of clauses. Use a capital letter if the conjunction begins a sentence.

when	until	although	if	since	because

We're going to the zoo ______________ Natalya hasn't been there.

I haven't been ______________ I went with Santi last May.

The chimpanzees weren't on view ______________ we went.

I wonder ______________ we'll see the chimpanzees today.

______________ Zac loves the zoo, he can't come with us.

Natalya won't be happy ______________ she sees chimpanzees.

Choose a topic that interests you. Write some **questions** that you have about the topic. Research your topic and create an **information report** that provides **statements** of information to answer your questions. Publish your report and present it to your class.

Unit 12 Revision

1 Write an interesting **noun group** for each of the following nouns. Use different kinds of adjectives.

__________________________ banana

__________________________ sea monster

__________________________ whale

__________________________ pizza

2 Choose a **possessive adjective** from the box for each **noun group** to show ownership.

our	its	my	their

My hat blew away and __________ brim got torn.

'Has someone taken __________ hat?' asked Katy.

They liked staying at __________ uncle's place.

We went to the NAIDOC celebrations with __________ brother.

3 Rewrite these word groups using an **apostrophe** to show possession.

The groceries belonging to the shoppers = __________________

The tea belonging to Mum = __________________

The dog belonging to Aunty Laura = __________________

The cars belonging to the teachers = __________________

The books belonging to the library = __________________

4 Circle the **relating verbs**.

My mother is a deep-sea diver.

My parents are swimmers.

My great-grandmother was Japanese.

This book belongs on my desk.

5 Rewrite each **sentence** in the **past tense**.

I will go to the shop soon.

____

I'll have soup for lunch.

____

6 Choose a **possessive pronoun** from the box to complete each sentence and show ownership.

his	hers	theirs	yours	mine	ours

My name's Hakim, what's ______________?

Hands off that chocolate, it's ______________!

Katie says the white jacket is ______________.

Josh admitted the mess was ______________.

I won't take a surfboard because Sadie and Liam will lend me ______________.

They already have tickets, so let's go and buy ______________.

7 Draw lines to show which **clauses** go together to make a **sentence**.

I'll clean my room	**but** she's still hungry.
Dad has a photo of Jonny	**because** he hasn't been fed yet.
I can play	**because** I have finished my homework.
The dog is hungry	**so** you can sleep over.
The cat has been fed	**when** he was a nipper.

8 Unjumble the **statements** and write them correctly on the lines. Hint! Each one has two **clauses** joined by a **conjunction**.

cycle to you can school if you a bike have

____

stayed home he was feeling although matt from school better

____

was stayed home feeling ill zara from school because she

____

he flu Dad stays home when symptoms has

____

Unit 13 Doing verbs, prepositional phrases, commands

This **imaginative** text is a recipe. It lists ingredients and uses **verbs** to tell what to do in the Method.

Frog Potion

How to turn a boring prince into a fabulous frog

Ingredients

- 1 strand of a prince's hair
- 1 hair off the back of the troll that lives under the bridge
- 1 tablespoon of ogre's swamp
- 1 scale from a mermaid's tail
- 1 dragon's toenail
- 1 pinch of sand from the bottom of the ocean

Method

1. Mix ingredients together.
2. Make the prince swallow the potion.
3. Close your eyes.
4. Chant three times to the prince:
   You are now a fabulous frog.

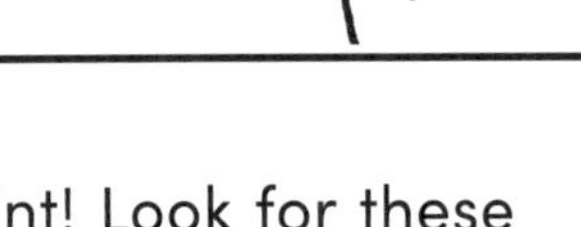

1 Read the *Frog Potion* recipe. Underline each **prepositional phrase**. Hint! Look for these prepositions: *of, off, under, from, into.*

2 Write four **doing verbs** used in the Method of the recipe.

____

3 Write ingredients that include **prepositional phrases** for an imaginative recipe of your own. Write the recipe's goal first. You might like to work with a partner.

How to ____________________________________

____

____

____

Grammar Rules! Student Book 4 (ISBN 9780655092520) © Tanya Gibb

Recipes require people to take action, so most steps in the method of a recipe begin with a **doing verb**.

4 Circle the **verbs** in the box that you might find in a normal recipe.

stir	type	bake	tell	throw	argue	yell	cook	blend	tell	fry

5 Create a Method for an imaginative recipe. Use some of the ingredients you wrote for question 3. Begin each step with a **doing verb**.

____

____

____

____

6 Edit and rewrite the text below as a numbered set of **commands** for a recipe.

Remember the rule on page 20.

Please mix together the flour and the butter and the sugar, if you like. Please be careful not to hurt yourself. If you spill any flour you might like to wipe it up so you don't make a mess. If you are tired you could have a rest and watch some television for a while. I don't know. Maybe you won't like these biscuits. You could probably add the sultanas and coconut now. Then you have to make little balls of the dough and put them on an oven tray and bake them for about 35 minutes.
I hope that's OK. Did you like them?

____

____

____

____

____

____

____

____

____

Work in a group. Share and discuss the ingredients and method you all wrote for questions 3 and 5. Create an imaginative recipe with the group to publish in a class recipe book that includes all the imaginative recipes.

Unit 14

Commands, adverbs

This text gives **instructions** to achieve a goal. Each instruction begins with a **verb** to tell class members what to do.

How to Work in a Group

- Present ideas clearly.
- Listen positively to others.
- Acknowledge and show respect for the opinions of others.
- Encourage everyone to contribute to discussions and decisions.
- Interact cooperatively.
- Give all group members equal opportunities to contribute.
- Allocate groups roles (e.g. making notes, reporting to the class) fairly.
- Be organised.
- Act responsibly.

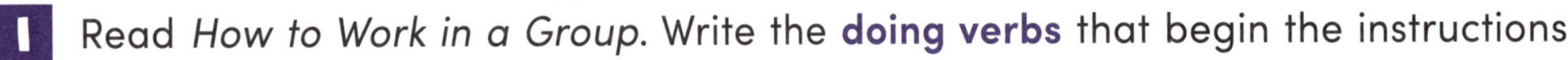

1 Read *How to Work in a Group*. Write the **doing verbs** that begin the instructions.

____

____

2 What does it mean to *listen positively to others?*

____

Adverbs tell time (*never, often, frequently*), place (*below, up, down, over*) or manner (*quickly, quietly, amazingly*). Adverbs modify adjectives (*very soft*), verbs (*slowly ate*) and other adverbs (*always late, really quickly*). Many adverbs end in *-ly*.

3 Write the five **adverbs** in *How to Work in a Group* that tell manner (how).

____

Grammar Rules! Student Book 4 (ISBN 9780655092520) © Tanya Gibb

4 Choose an **adverb** from the box to complete each **command**.

quickly	tunefully	proudly	slowly	carefully

Walk ______________ because we are running late.

Tread ______________ on the slippery rocks.

Eat ______________ or you'll get indigestion.

Sing ______________ so you'll be picked for the concert.

Stand ______________ for the photo.

5 Write an **adverb** on each blank line.

'I feel __________ that Erica should be team leader on this task,' said Bec.

'Erica would be a great team leader but she's had a turn __________, so it must be Kasey's turn __________,' suggested Manjit.

6 Replace the **prepositional phrases** with **adverbs** that tell manner (how). Write the new sentences.

Eat in a slow way. = Eat slowly.

Cross at a brisk pace. = ______________________________

The children played in a happy manner. = ______________________________

The dolphin jumped with ease over the boat. = ______________________________

Griffin laughed in a loud manner. = ______________________________

Write a set of **instructions** for a different classroom activity or game. Use dot points or number the steps if the sequence is important. Begin each step with a **doing verb** or an **adverb**.

Unit 15

Commands, doing verbs, proper nouns

This text gives **directions** from the writer's home to the public swimming pool. The directions are written in **numbered order**.

Directions to the Olympic Pool

From my house it is 1.5 kilometres to the Olympic swimming pool. These are the directions to get to the pool from my home:

1. Turn right out of my front gate.
2. Walk to the corner of the next street, which is Olsen Avenue.
3. Cross Olsen Avenue at the traffic lights.
4. Turn left into Olsen Avenue and walk two blocks until you come to the pedestrian crossing on Smith Street.
5. Cross Smith Street and turn right.
6. Walk one block to Charles Road.
7. Cross Charles Road at the pedestrian crossing and you will have arrived at the pool.

Tip The clearest way to write directions is to use **commands** and include **doing verbs**.

1 Circle the **doing verbs** in *Directions to the Olympic Pool*.

2 Choose a **doing verb** from the box to begin each **command**. Remember to begin the sentence with a capital letter.

walk	swim	catch	crawl	fly

__________ across the road.

__________ in a seaplane.

__________ the bus.

__________ around the island.

__________ through the tunnel.

3 Underline the **proper nouns** in *Directions to the Olympic Pool*.

Grammar Rules! Student Book 4 (ISBN 9780655092520) © Tanya Gibb

4 Complete each **command** with a **proper noun** from the box.

Aunty Freda	Dimitri	Dingle Street	Watson's	Tiggles

Say hello to ________________.

Deliver the letter to ________________.

Wash ________________.

Invite your friend ________________ to your party.

Buy bread at ________________ supermarket.

5 Rewrite the **statements** using capital letters for the **proper nouns**. Remember that a statement starts with a capital letter and ends with a full stop.

naarm (melbourne) is on the banks of the birrarung (yarra river)

____

uncle hien lives in toowong, which is a suburb of meanjin (brisbane)

____

leeawuleena ('sleeping water') is a beautiful area of lutruwita (tasmania)

____

the lake is on weebonenetiner country said bindi

____

6 Write a set of directions to get from your classroom to your school principal's office or a different location. Number each step. Use **doing verbs**.

____

____

____

____

____

Write a set of directions. Use your home as a starting point. Make sure you write the directions in logical order and use **doing verbs**. Remember that **proper nouns** (for street names, suburbs, towns and venues) have capital letters.

Unit 16

Clauses, sentences, nouns, pronouns, noun groups

This text is a **biography**. A biography tells about a person's life.

Isabel Letham, Surfie Legend

The first Australian to ride a surfboard was a woman named Isabel Letham. Isabel was fifteen when legendary Hawaiian surfer Duke Kahanamoku visited Australia and rode his surfboard in a surfing exhibition at Freshwater Beach. Isabel was on the beach watching the exhibition when Duke, also known as 'The Big Kahuna', asked for a volunteer to ride tandem with him. Isabel was chosen and became an instant celebrity in Australia and overseas. Isabel was involved in water sports all her life. She died in 1995 at age 96.

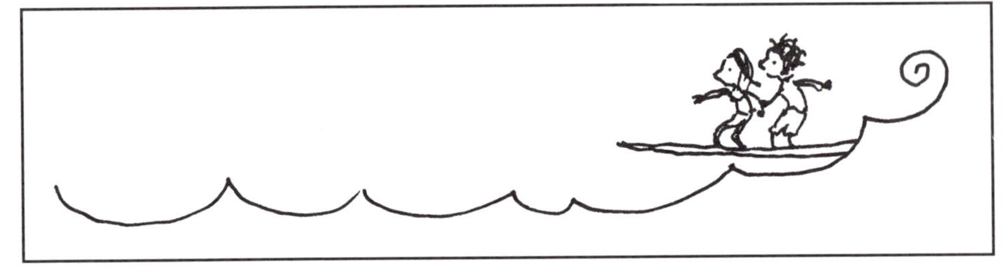

Rule

Nouns, **noun groups** and **pronouns** connect subject matter across a text.

<u>Albert Namatjira</u> was <u>a world famous artist</u>. He was <u>an Arrernte man</u>.

1 Read *Isabel Letham, Surfie Legend.* Underline the first word or word group in each sentence.

These are all words for __________________________.

2 Underline the first word or word group in each **sentence**.

Australia is famous for its surfing beaches.

The surf life saving movement started in 1907.

Surf Life Saving Australia celebrated its 100th anniversary in 2007.

Swimmers must look out for rips.

Grammar Rules! Student Book 4 (ISBN 9780655092520) © Tanya Gibb

The kinds of words used at the beginning of clauses or sentences highlight different aspects of meaning.

3 Write **sentences** beginning with the **word groups** below.

Ziggy and I ______________________________.

Slowly add ______________________________.

In the dark, dark forest ______________________________.

The night ______________________________.

Although ______________________________.

4 Underline the first word or word group in each **sentence**.

In Sydney, the Harbour Bridge is a famous tourist attraction.

Soccer practice is on Tuesdays.

The dog with four white feet is the cutest.

Occasionally, we go hiking in the National Park.

5 Underline the first word or word group in each **command**.

Practise piano every day.

Apply sunscreen liberally.

Swim between the flags.

Remember to wear a hat.

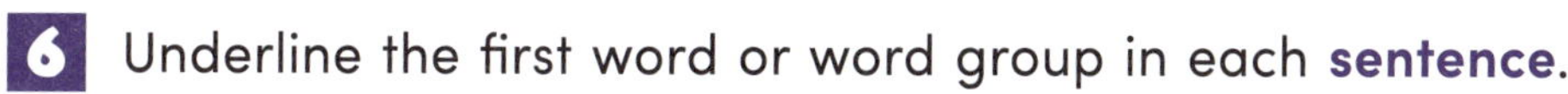

6 Underline the first word or word group in each **sentence**.

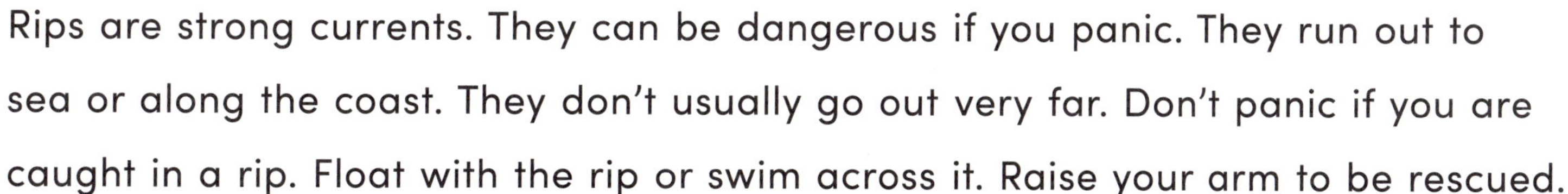

Rips are strong currents. They can be dangerous if you panic. They run out to sea or along the coast. They don't usually go out very far. Don't panic if you are caught in a rip. Float with the rip or swim across it. Raise your arm to be rescued.

Write a **biography** of someone you know. Interview them to gather information about their life. Write about events in time order. Use **nouns** and **pronouns** for the person at the beginning of sentences.

Unit **17** Helping verbs, verb tense, verb groups

Recycled Water

There is a fixed amount of water on earth. It all developed about four billion years ago and since that time has been recycled many millions of times in what is called the water cycle. In the water cycle, water evaporates from the oceans and rivers into the air. This evaporated water condenses into fog and mist, and forms clouds. The clouds move to the mountains and release water as rain, hail and snow. This water then forms rivers that flow to the ocean. Then the cycle begins again.

1 Read *Recycled Water*. Circle the **verbs** or **verb groups** below that are used in *Recycled Water*.

is	developed	is called	evaporates	dreams
condenses	jumped	move	release	joins
forms	dancing	flow	begins	has been recycled

A **verb group** contains a main verb and verbs that 'help' it.

is called *has been recycled*

Helping verbs (auxiliary verbs) can show **tense**.

future tense: *will be recycled*

past tense: *was recycled*

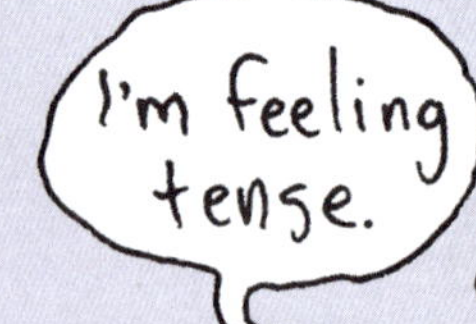

2 Underline the **verb group** in each sentence. Circle the **helping verbs**.

The water has been recycled.

It was developed a long time ago.

It is called the water cycle.

Water has been carried in clouds.

The clouds have moved to the mountains.

Grammar Rules! Student Book 4 (ISBN 9780655092520) © Tanya Gibb

Grammar Rules!

______________________'s Writing Log

1 Plan

What is the purpose of the text?
Who is the audience?
What type of text and text form will you use?
How can you enhance the presentation?
Gather ideas or research the topic, including using online and digital sources.

2 Draft

Gather and organise your ideas.
Use a graphic organiser or digital tools.
Compose your text.

3 Edit/Revise

Check your work for meaning, clarity and precision.
Is the structure and sequencing appropriate?
Check layout, paragraphing and sentence structures.
Check topic specific vocabulary.
Ask for help to improve meaning and precision.

4 Proofread

Check grammar and punctuation.
Check homophones are correct.
Use online dictionaries to check spelling.

5 Publish

Use layout and visual features.
Use digital tools.
Reflect on your work and your text.

Create symbols for a rating scale. Then each time you finish a piece of writing, record it in the log.

My rating scale

Symbol	Meaning
	Help!
	A good start.
	I have the basics covered.
	I'm beyond the basics.
	Brilliant!

Date	Write the title of your text.	Text purpose and structure	Audience
Write the date.	Write the title of your piece.	e.g. recount/ email	Who were you writing for or t

Do you need some ideas for other text forms to try? Look at the back page!

Language features	My rating	Where to next?
st the main grammar and other language atures that you used.	Record your rating.	What grammar could you try next? How could you improve your writing? Does your teacher have any comments?

I've tried these types of texts and text forms . . .

Narrative

- [ ] Story
- [ ] Comic
- [ ] Poem
- [ ] Retelling a story
- [ ] Other ____________________

Recount

- [ ] Letter/email
- [ ] News article
- [ ] A real or imagined event
- [ ] Imaginative recount
- [ ] Biography
- [ ] Other ____________________

Description

- [ ] Poem
- [ ] Letter
- [ ] Story
- [ ] Other ____________________

Informative

- [ ] Information report
- [ ] Biography
- [ ] Brochure/leaflet/poster
- [ ] Other ____________________

Procedure

- [ ] Recipe
- [ ] Instructions
- [ ] Rules
- [ ] Directions

Explanation

- [ ] Cycle diagram/flow chart
- [ ] Poster

Persuasion

- [ ] Debate
- [ ] Argument/speech
- [ ] Letter to editor
- [ ] Advertisement
- [ ] Poem
- [ ] Leaflet
- [ ] Other ____________________

Discussion

- [ ] Conversation
- [ ] Narrative dialogue
- [ ] Formal interview (TV, radio, guest speaker)
- [ ] Panel discussion
- [ ] Other ____________________

Response/Reflection

- [ ] Diary
- [ ] Review (book talk, film, concert, excursion)
- [ ] Poem
- [ ] Other ____________________

3 Use a **helping verb** from the box to complete each sentence. Then tick the **present** or **past** column after each one.

are	had	have	is	was	were

	Present	Past
The dog ________ moved the bone.		
We ________ eaten breakfast.		
We ________ making dinner.		
Margo ________ going out now.		
Jana ________ yelling this morning.		
Brett and I ________ running to the bus stop.		

4 Insert a **helping verb** to show that these actions will happen in the future.

We ____________ going to soccer practice later on.

Ozan ____________ having pizza for dinner.

The teacher ____________ mark the homework.

5 Draw a flow diagram to show the sequence of events in *Recycled Water*. Use extra paper.
A flow diagram uses arrows and labels. Show your diagram to others and discuss its accuracy and usefulness.

6 Change the **verb** form to show that these actions might happen in the future.

Tran (had walked) ______________ to the shop.

Frogs (have moved) ______________ into the new frog pond.

Myumi (had to run) ______________ home.

Quinn and Zoe (have read) ______________ that book.

Liam (went) ______________ to school today.

Write an **explanation** for a subject related to something you are doing in class. Use **present tense** for your **verb groups**. Use a flow diagram if it helps to clarify the explanation. Ask a peer to help edit your work.

Unit 18

Revision

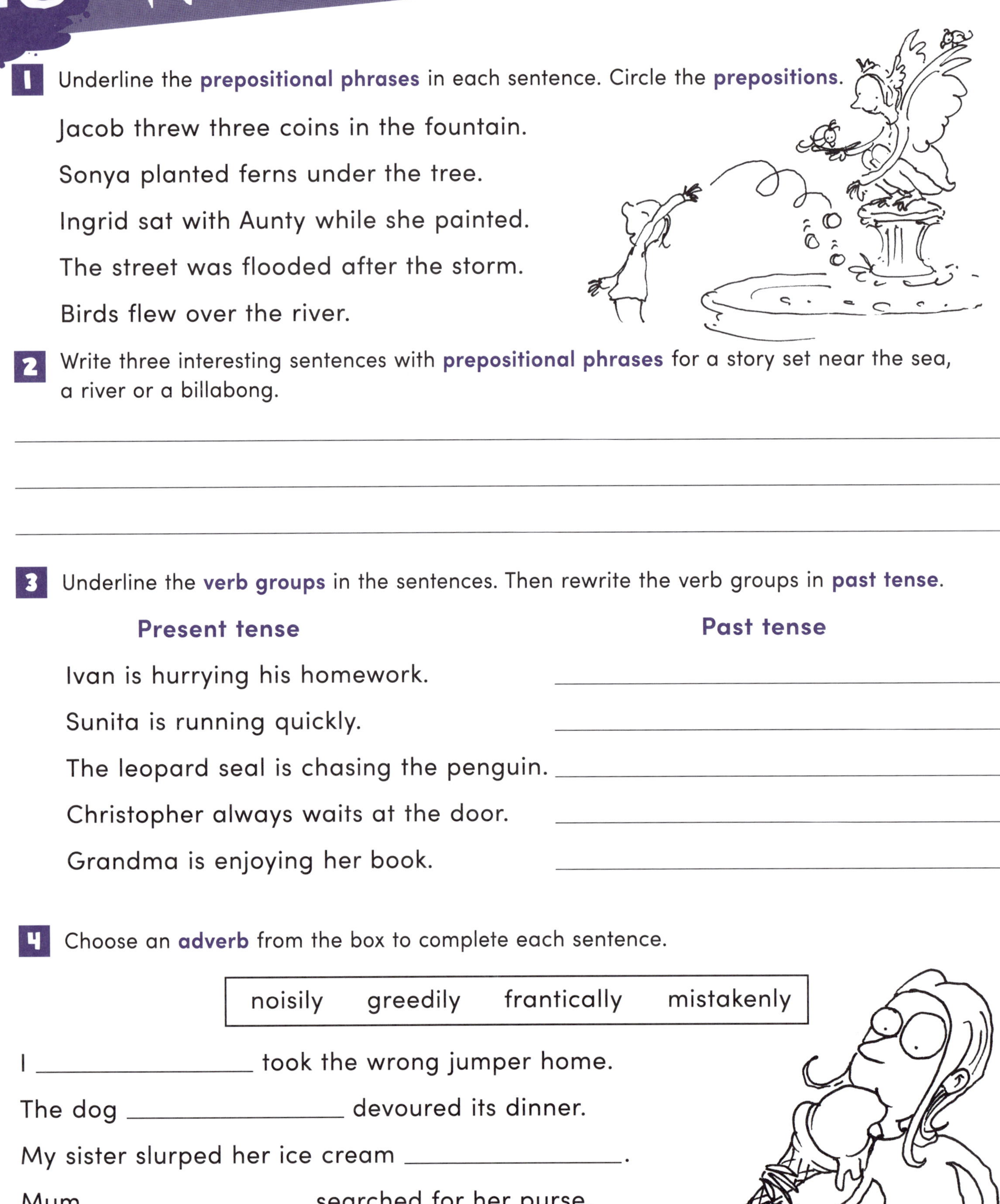

1 Underline the **prepositional phrases** in each sentence. Circle the **prepositions**.

Jacob threw three coins in the fountain.

Sonya planted ferns under the tree.

Ingrid sat with Aunty while she painted.

The street was flooded after the storm.

Birds flew over the river.

2 Write three interesting sentences with **prepositional phrases** for a story set near the sea, a river or a billabong.

____

____

____

3 Underline the **verb groups** in the sentences. Then rewrite the verb groups in **past tense**.

Present tense	Past tense
Ivan is hurrying his homework.	________________
Sunita is running quickly.	________________
The leopard seal is chasing the penguin.	________________
Christopher always waits at the door.	________________
Grandma is enjoying her book.	________________

4 Choose an **adverb** from the box to complete each sentence.

noisily	greedily	frantically	mistakenly

I ________________ took the wrong jumper home.

The dog ________________ devoured its dinner.

My sister slurped her ice cream ________________.

Mum ________________ searched for her purse.

Grammar Rules! Student Book 4 (ISBN 9780655092520) © Tanya Gibb

5 Write five **doing verbs** that you would use when giving directions.

____

6 Write two rules that apply in your classroom. Write each rule as a **command** beginning with a **doing verb**.

____

____

7 Rewrite each sentence. Replace each underlined phrase with an **adverb** that tells <u>manner</u> (how).

Cross the road <u>in a careful manner</u>. ______________________

The children played <u>in a noisy manner</u>. ______________________

The horse jumped <u>in a clumsy manner</u> over the fence.

____

Mum sang <u>in a loud manner</u>. ______________________

8 Underline the first word or word group in each sentence.

Barangaroo was a Cammeraygal woman of the Eora nation. She lived during the early days of colonisation in Sydney. She was well respected and influential.

What kinds of words did you underline? ______________________

9 Rewrite the **statements** correctly. Remember that a **statement** starts with a capital letter and ends with a full stop, and a **proper noun** begins with a capital letter.

barangaroo was married to bennelong ______________________

my teacher's name is ms hickman ______________________

debbie and lucy went together to frankie's house on shark island

____

the dog's collar stated its address as 101 hill street, fairlight

____

king neptune childcare centre is on trident street

____

Unit 19 Quoted and reported speech, emotive words

This is an online news report. Its headline is written to attract a reader's attention. It includes **quoted speech** and **reported speech**.

Just in | Watch live | World | Log in

Sewerage Wanted

Queensland farmers can't get enough sewerage. They say it makes great fertiliser.

Household sewerage is collected, treated and dried to make a product called biosolids. This is sold to farmers to improve soil quality, increase crop yield and help save water.

Farmer Jessie Allen has been using biosolids for a few years now and can't praise it highly enough. 'It's great stuff!' she exclaimed. 'We just can't get enough of it for our farm.'

Recycling human sewerage in this way means it does not go into the environment or the ocean.

1 Read *Sewerage Wanted*. What is the **main idea** in the report? Hint! This is the idea the writer or speaker wants you to believe or accept as true.

____

2 Underline the **reported speech** and circle the **quoted speech** in *Sewerage Wanted.*

3 Why would the news report have **quoted** Jessie Allen?

____

Speakers and writers can use **emotive words** to influence their audiences so that they respond emotionally to the topic.

The whales were slaughtered. *Try this decadent cake.*

The dolphins leapt joyfully.

4 Write five of the **words** or **phrases** used in *Sewerage Wanted* that should make readers feel positive about sewerage.

____

____

5 Does *Sewerage Wanted* make you feel favourable or unfavourable about biosolids? Explain.

____

6 Rewrite paragraph 3 of *Sewerage Wanted* as **reported speech**.

____

____

____

7 Fill in the missing adjectives.

If Monday is the first day of the week, Thursday is the ____________ day.

August is the ____________ month of the year.

The letter **i** is the ____________ letter of the alphabet.

Your ____________ birthday celebrates a decade of life.

Venus is the ____________ planet from the sun.

A centenary celebration marks the ____________ year of an event.

8 Write the **dialogue** of an **interview** between a news reporter (journalist) and a farmer. What extra **questions** could the farmer be asked about biosolids?

____

____

____

____

Comic strips use speech balloons for the quoted speech. They also use captions. Captions can help sequence events in time.
Meanwhile... Later that day...

9 Create a comic strip that shows a farmer using biosolids with great results. Use extra paper. Use captions for the time sequence.

Create an online **news report** for a topic of interest in your school or local community. Add **reported speech** as well as interview **quotes**. Use **words and phrases** that make readers respond emotionally to the topic.

Unit 20

Emotive words, personal pronouns, possessive adjectives

This **advertisement** uses **emotive words** and **commands** to persuade people to buy a product.

We Tank You

RAINWATER TANK

Install a rainwater tank.

Collect your own rainwater.

Beat water restrictions.

Help the environment.

Reduce your water bills – rainwater is free!

Call now on 1309 999 99 to arrange a free quote.

WE TANK YOU BECAUSE WE CARE

1 Read *We Tank You.* Circle the **doing verbs**.

2 Write a **synonym** for each **doing verb** in *We Tank You.*

_____________ your own rainwater.

_____________ a rainwater tank.

_____________ water restrictions.

_____________ now on 1309 999 99.

_____________ your water bills.

_____________ the environment.

3 Who might the **audience** be for *We Tank You?*

____

4 Write five **emotive words** used to appeal to the **audience** in *We Tank You.*

____

____

____

____

____

Advertisers sometimes use **personal pronouns** (*I, me, we, us, you*) and **possessive adjectives** (*your, our*) to make their advertisements seem more personal.

5 Write a **statement** after each **command** to state that you will obey.

Install a rainwater tank. We're going to install a rainwater tank.

Collect your own rainwater. ______________________________

Beat restrictions. ______________________________

Help the environment. ______________________________

Reduce your water bills. ______________________________

6 Complete each **command** to tell customers about other features of, or uses for, the rainwater tanks. Be as crazy as you like.

Use your tank for ______________________________

Hope your tank is ______________________________

Hug ______________________________

Catch ______________________________

7 What is the play on words in *We Tank You?*

____

8 Choose a **personal pronoun** from the box to complete each sentence. Use a capital letter if the pronoun begins a sentence.

I	me	we
you	us	

__________ had the first turn on the trampoline.

__________ had seaweed for dinner.

Mum gave __________ berries to share.

Did __________ see a crocodile?

Dad gave __________ a surfboard.

Write an advertisement to persuade your classmates to buy a classroom item such as a pen, a book, a chair, or any item you choose. Perform your advertisement for the class. Use body language, gestures and facial expressions to **persuade** your viewers.

Unit 21

Adjectival clauses, adjectives, simile

KATI THANDA-LAKE EYRE

Kati Thanda-Lake Eyre is in South Australia, in the middle of the desert, on Arabana Country. When it is completely filled with water it is the largest lake in Australia, but most of the time the area is a dry salt pan that looks like a shiny sparkling sea of white salt crystals.

When there's flooding rainfall in Queensland and the Northern Territory, a number of rivers carry the floodwaters hundreds of kilometres south to the lake. The lake has only been full four times since 1900, but every few years enough fresh water flows into the lake for it to become a spectacular oasis in the desert, teeming with wildlife.

This informative text is an **information report**. It uses **comparative adjectives** to describe the topic. It uses **conjunctions** to join clauses.

Conjunctions link clauses in a sentence by:

- adding information (*and*)
- comparing (*however, but, or*)
- showing one thing causes another (*so, because*)
- showing a time sequence (*when, then*).

1 Find and circle four **conjunctions** in *Kati Thanda-Lake Eyre*. Hint! There are two in each paragraph.

2 Add a **conjunction** to join the clauses by comparing.

Sometimes Kati Thanda is filled with water __________ mostly it is a dry salt pan.

Kati Thanda is rarely full __________ sometimes it has enough water to become a desert oasis.

An **adjectival clause** is a dependent clause that functions like an adjective. It helps describe a **noun**. It usually begins with *who, whom, which, that, when, why*.

My favourite T-shirt, <u>which is blue</u>, has a rip in it.

3 Circle the **adjectival clause** below.

The Lake Eyre dragon is a tiny lizard that walks on the heels of its feet so its toes don't get burnt.

Grammar Rules! Student Book 4 (ISBN 9780655092520) © Tanya Gibb

4 Use **conjunctions** to join each pair of sentences.

Lake Eyre dragons have sharp claws. The females can dig holes to lay their eggs.

____

Lake Eyre dragons live on Lake Eyre. Pebble dragons live on Lake Eyre.

____

Rule

Adjectives can be used to make comparisons. (*big-bigger-biggest*) Adjectives with more than two syllables need more or most to make comparisons. (*beautiful-more beautiful-most beautiful*)

5 Write the **adjective** used to make a comparison in *Kati Thanda-Lake Eyre*. ____________________

6 Complete the table. The first row is an example.

deep	deeper	deepest
lovely		
scary		
frightening		
funny		
salty		

7 Write more or most for the **adjectives** below.

The surgeon was ____________ capable than his colleague.

The surgeon was the ____________ capable surgeon in the hospital.

The athlete was the ____________ energetic on her team.

8 Copy the **simile** used in *Kati Thanda-Lake Eyre*. Hint! A simile is used to describe. It begins with *like* or *as*. (e.g. *The desert was like an alien moonscape.*)

____

Search the internet to find appropriate material to create an **information report** on a topic you are studying in class. Collect and insert a number of images and create a short slide show to present the information to the class.

Unit
22

Word play (neologisms, puns, spoonerism)

The speaker of this text has prepared a book talk to share opinions about a book and an author.

The BFG

My favourite book is The BFG by Roald Dahl.

In The BFG, there is a Big Friendly Giant who kidnaps Sophie from an orphanage. At first Sophie is frightened but she soon finds out that the BFG is friendly and protective and funny. The BFG doesn't eat 'human beans', so Sophie is safe with him but the other, not-so-friendly giants, Fleshlumpeater and Bonecruncher, are a bit scary.

I love Roald Dahl's invented words. For example, 'ucky-mucky' which means messy, and 'delumptious', which means delicious and scrumptious. 'Whizzpopping' is another useful, made-up word.

Dahl's stories always have interesting plots where the good or nice characters win in the end. I recommend all books by Roald Dahl, but especially The BFG.

By Bree

1 Read *The BFG*. Circle features of a **narrative** below that Bree mentions in her book talk. Then compare and discuss your choices with a partner.

plot character resolution setting language tension

2 What is the **purpose** of Bree's book talk and who is the **audience** for it?

____

3 What is Bree's purpose in each **paragraph** in the book talk?

1. ____
2. ____
3. ____
4. ____

4 Do you think Bree's book talk is effective and achieves her purpose? Explain your answer.

____

____

Grammar Rules! Student Book 4 (ISBN 9780655092520) © Tanya Gibb

5 Which **adjectives** are used to describe the BFG character in the book talk?

6 Write the **noun group** that describes Bonecruncher and Fleshlumpeater.

A **neologism** is a new or made-up word, or when a new meaning is given to an existing word or a word borrowed from another language. Neologisms are often accepted into common usage and might then be added to dictionaries.

Google *cyberspace* *spam* *webinar* *blogger*

7 Write the **neologisms** Bree loves in The BFG.

8 Lewis Carroll is another author who invented words. He invented *frabjous* for 'fabulous and joyous' and *chortle* for 'chuckle and snort'. Invent three **neologisms** and encourage friends and family use them.

A **pun** is wordplay where a word or phrase has more than one meaning. Puns are usually humorous. *Why did the circus clown spit out the lion? Because he tasted **funny**.*

A **spoonerism** is when the beginning sounds of words are swapped. *That's a pretty flutterby. I'm cakeing a bake. He's chewing the doors.*

9 Find or create a **pun** or a **spoonerism**. Write it here.

Prepare a book talk for the class. For a **fiction** book, describe whether it's fantasy, mystery, adventure, science fiction, realism, etc. Discuss **character**, **plot**, **setting**, **language** and any other features. For a **non-fiction** book, discuss **layout**, **subheadings**, **illustrations**, **photographs**, **index**, etc. Present your talk.

Unit 23

Dependent and independent clauses, conjunctions, verbs

This text uses **emotive language** and makes a call to action using **commands**.

Say NO to Plastic!

Plastic is a huge problem in the ocean.

Every year, thousands of sea animals die because of plastic. Animals get tangled in plastic and drown, or they choke on plastic when they think it's food. When an animal swallows plastic, it blocks the animal's digestive system and the animal starves to death.

Plastic lasts forever. In the ocean, over time, it breaks down into microscopic invisible particles, which fish unknowingly eat and, if we eat the fish, then we are eating plastic, too. Plastic never goes away.

Don't buy items wrapped in plastic. If you have to buy plastic, reuse it as often as you can and then recycle it. Don't throw it in the rubbish for landfill.

1 Read *Say NO to Plastic!* What is the **purpose** of each **paragraph**?

1. ______________________________

2. ______________________________

3. ______________________________

4. ______________________________

2 What is the **main idea** the author of *Say NO to Plastic!* wants you to accept?

____

3 Do you think the **illustration** strengthens or weakens the **main idea** of *Say NO to Plastic!*? Explain.

____

4 Circle the **personal pronouns** in *Say NO to Plastic!*.

Which **noun** does *it* refer to? ______________ Which **noun** does *they* refer to? ______________

Why do you think the writer uses the **personal pronouns** *we* and *you*?

____

Grammar Rules! Student Book 4 (ISBN 9780655092520) © Tanya Gibb

A comma separates an **independent clause** from a **dependent clause** in a **complex sentence** if the dependent clause comes first.

When it's my turn, I'm going to choose red.

While we were waiting, we saw some pelicans.

5 Circle the **conjunctions** and underline the **independent clauses** in these **complex sentences**.

Animals can choke to death when they swallow plastic.

Animals choke on plastic when they think it's food.

Whenever it ends up in the ocean, plastic is a threat to animals.

I always recycle plastic whenever I have to use it.

While we continue to make it, the environment is at risk from plastic.

When they think it's food, fish and turtles attempt to eat plastic.

6 Write four **verbs/verb groups** that begin **commands** in *Say NO to Plastic!*.

____

7 Underline the **verbs/verb groups** in paragraph 2 of *Say NO to Plastic!* Write them on the lines.

____

____

How might the choice of **verbs** in *Say NO to Plastic!* influence readers?

____

8 How do you feel about being told *you might be eating plastic?*

____

Write a persuasive text that uses **emotive words**. Choose any topic that you feel strongly about. Include **complex sentences**. Add an illustration. Publish your text and display it in your school or present it as a spoken text.

Unit 24 Revision

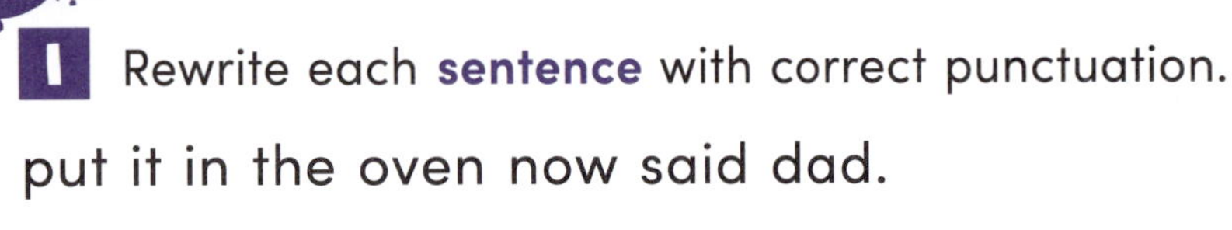

1 Rewrite each **sentence** with correct punctuation.

put it in the oven now said dad.

____

where are you going asked tahlee

____

stop shouted roberto

____

2 Circle the **verbs** and then underline any **dependent clauses**.

Although Paralympic events began in 1948, the Paralympic Games did not officially commence until 1960. Daphne Ceeney, who won medals for swimming, archery, javelin and shot put, was the only Australian female Paralympic competitor in the 1960 games.

3 Underline the **verbs/verb groups** in each sentence.

The first modern Olympics was held in Athens in 1896.

Australia has been competing in Olympic swimming since 1900.

Matthew Cowdrey is Australia's most successful Olympic swimmer, having won 23 Paralympic medals, including 13 gold.

Australian swimmers have proven their ability in international competition.

4 Change each **verb form** to show that the action happened in the past.

We (are running) ________________ to catch the bus.

I (am hopping) ________________ over the fence.

Minnie (is saying) ________________ to hurry up.

Johnny (does read) ________________ at bed time.

Trai (is chopping) ________________ the carrots.

Grammar Rules! Student Book 4 (ISBN 9780655092520) © Tanya Gibb

5 Write **past**, **present** or **future** after each sentence to show whether the event might or did take place.

We caught the ferry. ____________

I will catch the ferry. ____________

I've caught the ferry. ____________

I am on the telephone. ____________

I was on the telephone. ____________

I will phone her tomorrow. ____________

6 Use a more **emotive synonym** for the word in brackets in each sentence.

The whales were (killed) ____________ by the whaling ship.

The whale stranding was a (sad) ____________ sight.

Bees are (needed) ____________ for crop pollination.

The council ordered that the dog be (euthanised) ____________.

The teacher spoke (sternly) ____________ to the (child) ____________.

7 Choose the correct **comparative** and **superlative adjectives** from the box to complete each sentence.

bigger	biggest	slower	slowest	funnier	funniest

The tortoise is ____________ than the hare.

I read the ____________ book.

This book is ____________ than the other one.

The tortoise is the ____________ runner in the zoo.

My feet are ____________ than yours.

Its teeth are the ____________.

8 Write *more* or *most* on the lines.

One fish was ____________ colourful than the other.

This is the ____________ colourful fish.

Antarctica is ____________ remote than the Kimberley.

Punmu is one of the ____________ remote communities in Australia.

Unit 25

Subjective/objective language, inclusive language, noun groups

This text is from a television **interview**. The host asks the guest **questions** to entertain and inform viewers.

Cane Toads

Host: Good morning viewers and welcome to our guest, Lauren Walker.

Guest: Thank you for having me.

Host: What do you want to tell viewers about cane toads?

Guest: They were imported to Australia from Hawaii in 1935 to eat the cane beetles that were destroying the sugarcane crops in Queensland, but they have become a feral pest across the northern half of Australia, eating anything they can swallow.

Host: Why are experts so worried about the cane toad?

Guest: The cane toad has no natural predator in Australia and our native animals are defenceless against it. It's also poisonous to our animals and has been linked to the extinction of predatory native species, such as the northern quoll.

Host: That's extremely disturbing. What's being done about it?

Objective language is factual and unbiased: *German Shepherds are used by the police.* **Subjective language** shows a point of view or bias: *German Shepherds are aggressive.*

1 Read *Cane Toads*. Is the host **subjective** or **objective** about the topic? ______________________

Explain. ____

2 Circle the **noun groups** and **pronouns** used for cane toad/cane toads in *Cane Toads*.

Write the noun group used for cane toad that does not say 'cane toad'. ______________________

3 What does *That* refer to in the last line of *Cane Toads*?

____

4 In which two ways can a cane toad harm native species? ______________________

____

5 Why doesn't the cane toad have any *natural predators* in Australia?

____

Grammar Rules! Student Book 4 (ISBN 9780655092520) © Tanya Gibb

A **noun group** can include another noun used to **classify** the main noun.
a cane toad *many water birds* *the kitchen sink*

6 Find and write two **noun groups** that **classify** in *Cane Toads*. Don't use 'cane toads'.

---

7 Circle the **nouns** used to **classify** in each noun group below.

a very long but exciting tennis match a curious humpback whale

a cotton shirt a guitar player a cheese sandwich

8 Find and write the **emotive** terms used by the guest speaker in *Cane Toads*.

---

9 The interview in *Cane Toads* uses **formal language**. How might the two people greet each other in an **informal** situation? Write their greetings as quoted speech.

Inclusive language is language that is respectful and inclusive of diversity. Language should also be nonviolent.
First Nations Australian *police officer* *waiter*
older Australian *person with disability*
Use the pronoun 'they' for a person who has not identified their gender to you or who chooses to be identified as 'they' rather than 'he' or 'she.'

10 Circle the **inclusive** or **nonviolent** term in each pair.

homeless person/person without housing wheelchair user/wheelchair-bound person

the elderly/older adults fireman/firefighter is mentally ill/has a mental illness

waitress/waitstaff Take your best shot./Give it a go.

You're killing it./You're doing a great job.

Do some research about a feral animal (e.g. a rabbit, cat, fox, camel, buffalo, pig). Write a set of **formal interview** questions about the animal for television. Begin the interview with an **Acknowledgement of Country**.

Unit **26** Modal verbs, modal adverbs

This news report is informative. It uses **emotive words** to engage readers.

Lucky to be Alive!

Residents of Bilkington were forced to climb onto their roofs overnight as raging floodwaters surged over riverbanks and through the town.

Many homes in Bilkington are underwater today and extensive flooding is likely to continue for the next 24 hours. Roads are impassable, so the town will remain isolated for days. Emergency Services are delivering critical supplies by air.

Local resident Ted Egan said that because of climate change there will be more severe and frequent flooding in the future and the town will suffer again.

Police have reminded people that flooded roads are extremely dangerous. People must not drive on or attempt to cross flooded roads.

1 Read *Lucky to be Alive!* Write the **emotive words** or phrases used in the first paragraph.

________________ ________________ ________________

2 Find **synonyms** in *Lucky to be Alive!* for the following words.

blocked ________________ swept ________________

serious ________________ large-scale ________________

inaccessible ________________ submerged ________________

3 Imagine you lived in Bilkington. What might **you** say to a news reporter about the events?

____

____

4 Write the **noun groups** in *Lucky to be Alive!* that refer to people. This is who the report tells about.

____

5 News reports tell **who**, **what**, **where**, **when**, **how** and/or **why** events unfolded. What has happened to residents in Bilkington?

____

6 Rewrite these sentences with correct punctuation.

mr egans daughter was rescued by a neighbour in a tinnie

____

essential supplies include food water medicine batteries and animal fodder

____

the bureau has predicted considerable rainfall until tuesday

____

mary egan said I managed to rescue my cat budgie photo albums and important documents before climbing up to the roof

____

____

Tip

Modal verbs (also called modal auxiliaries) (e.g. *should, might, must, will, can't*) and **modal adverbs** (e.g. *possibly, probably, always, rarely*) are used to make statements more or less forceful, certain, likely or convincing.

You probably should help. You definitely must help.

7 Rewrite each sentence to express **more certainty**.

The town might not cope. ______________________

The council will likely help. ______________________

Homes could be ruined. ______________________

People will possibly be angry. ______________________

It might rain on Friday. ______________________

Write a **news article** about a real or fictitious incident in your local area. Make sure you tell **who**, **what**, **where**, **when**, **how** or **why** the incident occurred. Use interview **quotes** or **reported speech** and **emotive language**.

Unit 27

Subjective/objective language, noun-verb agreement

These two texts deal with the same aspect of history but have different **authors** and **purposes**.

Text 1

Missing from History

Matthew Flinders gets the credit,
but what of Bungaree?
Bungaree sailed with Flinders;
was his
cultural guide
and negotiator.
Bungaree – the first **Australian**
circumnavigator –
a Kuringgai man!
Where is his name in the history
books?
Where is the statue to honour him?
No fame or glory for Bungaree.
Only fame and glory for Flinders –
the first English man
to circumnavigate Australia
(with his cat named Trim).

Text 2

Matthew Flinders

In 1803, Matthew Flinders, a British navigator and mapmaker, became the first person to circumnavigate mainland Australia.

There are statues of Trim in England and Australia. This one is outside the Mitchell Library in Sydney.

Source: www.nma.gov.au

1 Read *Missing from History*. What is the **main idea** in the poem?

____

2 What might a *cultural guide* and *negotiator* have done for Matthew Flinders?

____

____

3 What might *fame* and *glory* mean for Matthew Flinders?

____

To judge if an online **reference source** is reliable, check for '.edu' or '.gov'. These sources are usually reliable. Other sources might be reliable but check for author bias and that the date of publication is recent. Use other sources to confirm any information.

Grammar Rules! Student Book 4 (ISBN 9780655092520) © Tanya Gibb

4 Can you judge that the **source** of the statement Text 2 *Matthew Flinders* is likely to be reliable? Explain.

____

5 Why do you think the poet of *Missing from History* asks questions?

____

6 Write **subjective** or **objective** after each statement.

The government is considering raising the dam wall. ______________

Raising the dam wall will destroy pristine wilderness areas. ______________

Sally has nightmares that trouble her. ______________

Sally's complaints are annoying. ______________

Bungaree was a Kuringgai man. ______________

Bungaree was the first Australian to circumnavigate mainland Australia. ______________

7 Compare Texts 1 and 2.

How are they the same? ____

How are they different? ____

Rule

A **verb** needs to agree with a **noun** in number.
Singular number: *The shark lives... It lives...*
Plural number: *The sharks live... They live...*

8 Rewrite each sentence. Change the underlined noun to singular. Remember to also change the verb to suit the noun.

The children run past the teachers. The child runs past the teachers.

The dogs eat dog biscuits. ____

The babies cry for hours. ____

The authors visit all schools in the district. ______________________________

____

Is there a statue or a memorial in your local community? What is it for? Write a **poem** that gives your opinion about the subject of the statue or any community issue of interest to you. Read your poem to class members.

This **formal** speech uses **persuasive** statements to present a point of view. **Connectives** link the arguments.

Too Cruel!

Good afternoon, Principal Patel, teachers and students.
I begin by acknowledging the Dja Dja Wurrung people of the Kulin Nation, Traditional Owners of this land on which we meet.

I'm speaking against the keeping of dolphins and whales in captivity.

Firstly, most dolphins and orcas are captured from the wild, so separation from their families and their pods is heartbreaking. These are highly social animals, and they suffer from loneliness and boredom in captivity.

Secondly, dolphins and whales swim hundreds of kilometres a day in the wild, and so being confined to a swimming pool must be torture for them.

Additionally, dolphins and whales are extremely intelligent. Some scientists believe that dolphins are the second smartest animal on the planet, after humans. They love to play and explore and interact.

Don't pay to see dolphins or whales in captivity. It's cruel to keep these animals in zoos, theme parks and aquariums.

Thank you.

1 What is the **main idea** in the text?

____

2 Read *Too Cruel!* Do you think the **title** suits the text? Explain.

____

3 What is the function of each **paragraph** after the Acknowledgement of Country in *Too Cruel!*?

1. ______________________________
2. ______________________________
3. ______________________________
4. ______________________________
5. ______________________________

Grammar Rules! Student Book 4 (ISBN 9780655092520) © Tanya Gibb

Connectives link sentences and paragraphs across a text.
firstly *then* *therefore* *however* *nevertheless* *in addition*
Conjunctions are a kind of connective.

4 Underline the **connectives** in *Too Cruel!*. These link the paragraphs in a logical sequence.

5 Use a **conjunction** from the box to join each pair of sentences. Tick the column to show the function of the conjunction in each sentence.

so	because	however	but

I love whales. I don't like eels.

____

Whales migrate to and from Antarctica. They can feed on krill.

____

____

I like sharks. I prefer whales.

____

I love whales. They are gentle giants.

____

Function	
to compare	to show cause

6 Circle the **emotive words** in *Too Cruel!*. How do these emotive words make you feel about the topic?

____

____

Create a speech that presents an **argument** to the class. Choose any topic you feel strongly about. When presenting your speech, use your **voice** to sound convincing. Use **pitch**, **pace**, **tone**, **pause** and **emphasis** as well as **body language**.

Unit 29

Suffixes, subordinating conjunctions

This is an information report. It uses **verb groups** to show actions (**doing verbs**) and relationships (**relating verbs**).

Tsunami

A tsunami is a long, tall ocean wave or a series of waves. Tsunamis are mainly caused by earthquakes in the sea floor. They can also occur when a volcano erupts. When Mount Krakatoa erupted in Indonesia in 1883, it caused a tsunami that grew to 40 metres high on the coast of Indonesia. When that tsunami reached the north-west coast of Australia, it was still six metres high.

Tsunami waves quickly move out and away from where the earthquake or volcano occurred. Sometimes there is only one tsunami. Sometimes there is a series of tsunamis. The north-west coast of Australia is the most likely place on Australia's coast to be hit by a tsunami.

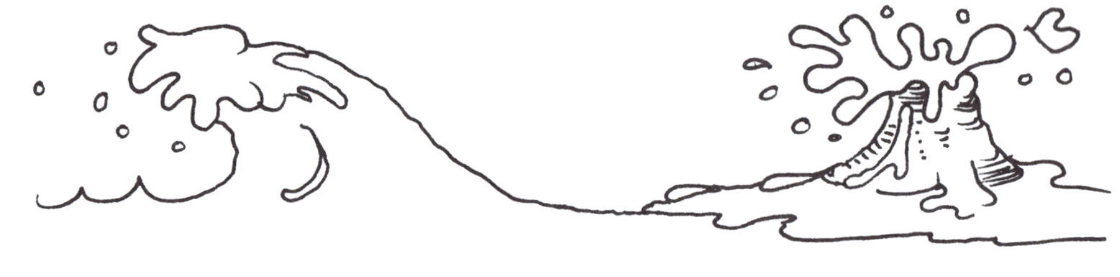

1 Read *Tsunami*. Find and circle the following **verbs** and **verb groups**.

is	are mainly caused	erupted	caused		
can also occur	is	is reached	was	move	
to be hit	erupts	grew	occurred	is	

Remember the rule on page 40.

2 Write three **adverbs** in *Tsunami* that end in *-ly*. ______________________

3 Which **noun group** in *Tsunami* tells what a tsunami is? ______________________

4 What causes tsunamis? ______________________

5 Where might Australians see a tsunami? ______________________

Grammar Rules! Student Book 4 (ISBN 9780655092520) © Tanya Gibb

Suffixes, helping (auxiliary) verbs and **modal verbs** show **verb tense.**
erupt: erupts, is erupting, erupted, didn't erupt, has erupted, might erupt

6 Add **suffixes** to write the different forms of these **regular verbs.**

Base form	Present tense	Past tense	Past tense with helping verb
walk	I am ______	I ______	______
receive	I am ______	I ______	______
laugh	I am ______	I ______	______
call	I am ______	I ______	______
decide	I am ______	I ______	______
think	I am ______	I ______	______

7 Circle the **verb/verb group** in each clause and add a **conjunction** from the box to join the clauses. Use a capital letter if the conjunction begins the sentence.

since	whether	although	when	whenever	unless	while

______ there is a volcanic eruption, volcanologists are keen to study it.

______ Krakatoa erupted, the ash cloud went 27 km into the sky.

You can't go on the excursion ______ you have a permission note.

______ Krakatoa was erupting in 1883, the explosions could be heard in Perth.

There's over a million volcanoes in the ocean ______ most are now extinct.

Swimming training is on today ______ it's raining or not.

______ Yuri heard about Krakatoa, he's become fascinated by tsunamis.

A tsunami is different from a tidal wave. Research tidal waves (or earthquakes, volcanoes or another natural phenomenon that interests you). Write an **information report**. Use digital tools to present the information to the class.

Unit 30 Revision

1 Circle the **verb/verb group** in each sentence.

Gina quietly waited in the queue at the canteen.

Zara raced over the finish line in first place.

The wombat slowly waddled through the long grass, chomping as it went.

Passengers are required to carry their own luggage.

Fred couldn't understand the problem.

Parent plovers fiercely protect their chicks.

2 Add a **main clause** to each dependent clause below to complete each sentence.

While Skye was waiting, ______________________________.

After Nikita finished, ______________________________.

Although Arabella enjoys mystery novels, ______________________________.

Whenever Frankie takes Sam hiking, ______________________________.

When every student has finished the test, ______________________________.

3 Rewrite each sentence so that the events have occurred in the past.

Mahsa always wakes when the rooster crows.

____

Evey is planning to build a possum house.

____

Jeremy will drive Meaghan to the train station.

____

'I am researching octopuses,' said Louella.

____

4 Use a **conjunction** from the box to complete each sentence.

but	until	and	so	because

Meg will wait ______________ Pia has finished dinner.

Leila ______________ Eric are coming to dinner.

Hugo likes broccoli ______________ Ireni doesn't.

I'll stay inside ______________ it's raining.

Uncle Hal can't eat sugar ______________ we bought him artificial sweetener.

5 Circle the **inclusive** or **nonviolent** term in each pair.

Hi guys./Hi everyone. the Chair/the Chairman a male nurse/a nurse

disabled person/person with a disability old people/older people

policeman/police officer is a nut case/is mentally ill mankind/humankind

Let's bite the bullet./Let's get this done. betrayed/stabbed in the back

Set-up will require 5 man-hours./Set-up will require 5 hours.

Take your best shot./Give it a go. You're killing it./You're doing a great job.

6 Rewrite each statement to make it **very certain**, **likely** or **definite**.

The school debating team might have a chance at winning the competition.

____

Rachel could possibly cycle to school if she gets a new bike.

____

7 Rewrite each sentence with correct punctuation. Don't forget to begin **proper nouns** with a capital letter.

my friend gemma is travelling to victoria for the school holidays in december

____

____

the great barrier reef is beautiful but it is under threat

____

cassowaries live at cape tribulation in north queensland

____

Unit 31 Connectives, modal verbs and adverbs

This text is **persuasive**. The writer/speaker wants you to agree with their **point of view**. **Reasons** or **evidence** support their **argument**.

Vote Against School Swimming

I think that schools should not have swimming as a school sport.

Firstly, I believe that anyone in Australia who wants to swim or who likes swimming will swim outside of school anyway, so why waste school time doing things that everyone can already do?

Secondly, swimming during school hours increases the risk of skin cancer. We should not expose children to the sun at swimming pools.

Furthermore, I feel that the time spent swimming would be better spent doing other, more important, activities like spelling and mathematics.

Because of the reasons I've stated, I believe you should vote against swimming as a school activity.

1 What is the **main idea** of *Vote Against School Swimming*?

Summarise the three reasons the writer/speaker uses to support their argument.

2 In *Vote Against School Swimming*, underline the **connectives** that help to **sequence** the arguments.

Remember the rule on page 63.

3 Write the **thinking verbs** used in *Vote Against School Swimming*.

4 When making an **argument**, it is important to express **certainty**. Tick each statement that expresses certainty.

- ☐ We cannot waste school time on swimming.
- ☐ Swimming lessons are great fun.
- ☐ It's possible that our school could win at the carnival.
- ☐ I know many children who swim on the weekend.
- ☐ People might already swim outside of school.
- ☐ We must make children wear sunscreen.
- ☐ We could offer sunscreen for those who want to use it.

5 Think of two other reasons to support the **argument** to vote against school swimming. Express the reasons strongly and with certainty.

____

____

6 Write the **argument** to vote FOR school swimming. Write an introduction and then the opposite argument of each argument summarised in question 1. Add any other supporting statements you can think of. Write a concluding statement. Plan your argument here, then publish it online, on extra paper or as a speech. Use **connectives** to structure your argument.

____

____

____

____

____

____

____

____

Write an **argument** for or against something you feel strongly about. Use **connectives** like *firstly* and *secondly* to structure your argument. Use **modal verbs** and **adverbs** such as *must*, *should* and *definitely* to show you are certain of your opinions. Use **thinking verbs** to express your opinions.

Unit 32

Pronouns, dependent and independent clauses

This text presents a **glossary** of First Nations words and their meanings.

First Nations Words

There are hundreds of Australian First Nations languages. Here are some First Nations words that are used in Australian English.

- Bilby – a word from the Yuwaalaraay language that means long-nosed rat
- Billabong – a word from a Wiradjuri language that means lake
- Canberra – from the local Ngunnawal language, a word that means meeting place (Canberra is the capital of Australia and the city where our parliament meets.)
- Kangaroo – a Guugu Yimithirr word for a marsupial with long hind limbs
- Wallaroo – a Dharug word for a mountain kangaroo
- Wombat – a Dharug word for a burrowing marsupial
- Yidaki – the Yolngu name for a didgeridoo. The didgeridoo was invented over a thousand years ago by Australia's First Peoples but 'didgeridoo' is not a word in any First Nations language.
- Yowie – a Yuwaalaraay word for a hairy monster

1 What is the **main idea** in the text?

____

2 Why is the term *local* used in dot point 3?

____

3 Circle the **noun group** in the first paragraph of *First Nations Words* that includes a number adjective.

4 What does *that* refer to in dot point 1 of *First Nations Words*?

____

What does *that* refer to in dot point 2? ______________________________

What does *that* refer to in dot point 3? ______________________________

5 Circle two **prepositional phrases** in the sentence below.

Australia's First Nations peoples have lived in Australia for thousands of years.

6 Circle what *It* refers to in the sentences below.

An Acknowledgement of Country is a statement that anyone can make. It shows that they are aware of the Traditional Custodians of the land they are on.

Who does the personal pronoun *they* refer to? ______________________________

Rule

Some **dependent clauses** function like **adverbs** to tell place (where), time (when) or manner (how).

They played in the waves until they were exhausted. (time)

I ran as fast as I could. (manner)

7 Underline the **dependent (adverbial) clause** in each sentence.

Year 4 will sing the national anthem once the Welcome to Country is finished.

Uncle James will perform the Welcome to Country as proudly as he can.

Year 5 will recite a poem by Henry Lawson after Year 4 has finished singing.

Before she goes to school, Kaila practises the clarinet.

8 Circle the **verbs** and then underline the **independent (main) clause** below.

A Welcome to Country is a ceremony that is performed by a First Nations Elder to welcome visitors to their traditional lands.

9 Write an **independent (main) clause** for each **dependent clause**.

______________________________ as quickly as she could.

Before the race began, ______________________________.

______________________________ after we've eaten lunch.

______________________________ unless she finishes her homework.

Wherever Casper goes ______________________________.

Try it yourself!

Work with a partner or in a group. Create a **glossary** of First Nations words. They can be words used in English or other words you find. Illustrate your glossary. Display it in your class or library or publish it online.

Unit 33

Emotive words, clauses, determiners

This leaflet article is **informative.** It begins with an opening statement. It provides background information about a problem. It concludes with a recommendation for action.

FLOODS AND WILDLIFE

Severe flooding has severely impacted wildlife over recent months.

Floodwaters can drive wildlife into urban areas where they face dangers from cars and pets. Tragically, a mother kangaroo, trying to escape fast-flowing floodwaters during the most recent flooding event, was hit by a car and killed. Luckily, the driver rescued the kangaroo's joey, which is now being cared for by a wildlife rescue group.

Floodwaters can trap wombats in their burrows and they often drown. If they do manage to escape their flooded burrows, they have difficulty finding shelter or food. Rescue groups sometimes erect temporary shelters for wombats in flooded areas or remove the wombats into care until their home range is clear of floodwater.

Contact a wildlife rescue group in your local area if you notice a native animal in distress.

1 What is the **purpose** of the text *Floods and Wildlife*?

2 Who is the intended **audience**?

3 Underline the **dependent clause** in the final paragraph of *Floods and Wildlife*.

4 Find and write three **compound words** used in *Floods and Wildlife*.

5 Find and write the **emotive words** used in the text.

Grammar Rules! Student Book 4 (ISBN 9780655092520) © Tanya Gibb

6 Circle the **verbs** in the complex sentences below. Underline the **independent clauses**.

Rescue groups sometimes erect temporary shelters for wombats in flooded areas until their home range is clear of floodwater.

The driver rescued the kangaroo's joey, which is now being cared for by a wildlife rescue group.

Rule

Determiners are words that identify or point out particular **nouns** or **noun groups**. *those apples, this apple*
Articles (*a, an, the*) are determiners.

7 What does the **noun group** *these situations* mean in the sentence below?

Many native animals are at risk during floods and these situations are becoming more frequent due to climate change. ____________________

8 Find **synonyms** in *Floods and Wildlife* for the following words.

impermanent ____________________ sadly ____________________ flee ____________________

built-up ____________________ incident ____________________ build ____________________

observe ____________________ trouble ____________________

9 Rewrite the **reported speech** as **quoted speech**.

The most rescued native animal in Australia is a bird, according to Tariq Sims.

____

10 Circle the **emotive words** and **phrases** below.

Animals that become entangled in barbed wire fencing die slowly and painfully. If they are rescued, they usually have to be put down because their injuries are too horrific to enable them to survive.

How does the writer of the **description** want you to feel? ____________________

Do some research about ways to help animals during natural disasters, such as droughts. Create a poster, leaflet or multimodal text for display in your school, shopping centre or community.

Unit 34

Flashback, tension, determiners

The Quest to Save Allura

Giselle and Eamon rode slowly towards the enormous wooden gates that blocked access across the dark moat. They were here to beg the Council of Elders for help.

Giselle was frightened. She could tell Eamon was too by the grim look on his face and his white knuckles gripping the reins. She knew Walnut could also sense Eamon's fear. He snorted white steam into the early morning chill and shook his head. The air was silent… holding its breath.

Creeeeak! The giant gates slowly began to open. The sound caused Giselle to remember the last time they'd ridden through these gates, when their father had lost his life. Now she and Eamon faced the same threat.

This extract from a **narrative** is told from the perspective of one of the characters. It describes the setting and includes a **flashback** that gives readers a reason for the characters' feelings.

Rule The plot in a narrative needs to have **tension** or **conflict** so that readers want to read on and find out what happens to the characters.

1 Write the **noun groups** used in *The Quest to Save Allura* that help you imagine the **setting**.

____

____

2 Circle the words in *The Quest to Save Allura* that give the story **atmosphere** or **mood**.

Rule A **flashback** is a literary device that allows the narrator to explain something that happened in the past. A flashback helps readers understand a character and the current situation in the plot.

3 What is the flashback in *The Quest to Save Allura*?

____

4 How can a reader tell that Giselle and Eamon are right to be frightened? Explain.

____

Grammar Rules! Student Book 4 (ISBN 9780655092520) © Tanya Gibb

5 Write a flashback for this extract from a story.

Henry suddenly noticed Clem ahead of him on the footpath. He immediately stopped and started backing away. He didn't want Clem to see him. The last thing he wanted was a confrontation with Clem. A few months ago...

____

____

____

6 What does the air do in *The Quest to Save Allura* that makes you feel it's human?

____

7 Rewrite the events in paragraph 2 of *The Quest to Save Allura* using Eamon to tell the story.

____

____

____

8 Use a **determiner** (*this, that, these, those*) on each line. Use a capital letter if the determiner begins a sentence.

__________ cold weather is hard on Grandma's health.

__________ mandarins are sweeter than __________ mandarins.

__________ painting is more colourful than __________ painting.

9 Write an **adverb** that tells manner (how) on each line.

__________, he sat down on the mountain peak.

__________, they trudged for hours through the dunes.

__________, they photographed the bilby before it hopped away.

__________, the humpback cavorted in the ocean depths.

Write a story. Plan your **plot** so there is **tension** and conflict between **characters** or between characters and their environment. Describe the **setting** so readers can imagine it. Tell readers how the characters feel and what they are thinking.

Unit 35 Revision

1 Complete the chart.

Base form	Past tense	Future tense
see	I ________	________
buy	I ________	________
jump	I ________	________
tickle	I ________	________
think	I ________	________

2 Rewrite each sentence with correct punctuation and capital letters.

can anyone recommend a good book asked ellen

____

have you read the first scientists by sorey tutt asked adam

____

ive read it declared reba

____

i got it for my birthday in october said adam

____

3 Add a **clause** to complete each sentence.

Until it rains, ________________________________.

Although I like blackberry jam, ________________________.

________________________________, then we can go to the park.

If you hold Maggie's hand, ________________________.

Grammar Rules! Student Book 4 (ISBN 9780655092520) © Tanya Gibb

4 Underline the **connectives**.

I don't like television. Firstly, I get bored just sitting on the couch. Secondly, the ads are really annoying. Finally, there are never any good shows on!

5 Circle the **verbs/verb groups** in each sentence.

Alexi was pleased that her teacher liked her poem.

Otto asked his mother if he could visit the library after school.

The leaves slowly drifted to the ground.

The koala that was rescued from the dog is recovering well.

'People should keep their dogs on leads,' declared Lulu angrily.

6 Add one or more interesting **prepositional phrases** to complete each sentence.

The children struggled ____.

Henry stumbled ____.

Jane helped Noah ____.

Will likes coffee ____.

7 Underline the **nouns** and **noun groups**.

Zan could barely see the ground in the pale moonlight.

The eastern curlew flies thousands of kilometres between Australia and Russia.

Heat the coconut oil in a large saucepan and fry the chopped onion.

Buy Australian grown and support Aussie farmers.

Bananas provide magnesium for good health.

We must reduce our reliance on plastic and help the environment.

8 Write **subjective** or **objective** after each statement.

Olives taste disgusting on pizzas. ________________

Pristine wilderness areas will be destroyed if the development goes ahead. ____________

The forest is home to the critically endangered swift parrot. ________________

Sarah needs to practise her handwriting. ________________

Ms Nguyen is a kind teacher. ________________

The Boyds have adopted a greyhound. ________________

Glossary

Look at the page number in the circle to find more information about the rule or tip.

adjective............a word that tells more about a **noun** (15)
- *adjectival clause* (48)
- *to describe* (15) (16)
- *for possession* (25)
- *to compare or show preference* (49)
- *for number or quantity* (15)

adverb................a word/word group that modifies a **verb**, **adjective** or another adverb (34)
- *adverbial clause* (71)
- *can tell time, place or manner* (34)
- *modal adverbs* (59)

antonym............a word that means the opposite of another word (16)

article.................(*a, an, the*) used in front of a **noun** or at the beginning of a **noun group** (15)

clause.................a unit of meaning that includes a **verb** (11)
- *adjectival clause* (48)
- *dependent clauses* (29) (71)
- *adverbial clause* (71)
- *independent clause* (11) (26)

comma..............a punctuation mark that separates items in a series (20)
- *dependent clauses* (53)
- *quoted speech in a sentence* (12)

command..........a sentence that tells someone to do something (20)

compound sentence.....a sentence consisting of two **independent clauses** (11)
- *joined by a coordinating conjunction* (26)

conjunction.......a word than joins **clauses** in a sentence (11) (26) (29) (48)
- *coordinating (joins independent clauses in a compound sentence)* (26)
- *subordinating (joins a dependent clause in a complex sentence)* (29)

connective.........a word or words (including **conjunctions**) that link ideas through a text through reason, addition, time or comparison (63)

contraction........a word made by combining two or more words and leaving letters out (21)

determiners......words that identify or point out (73)

emotive words..words chosen to make readers or listeners feel a certain way about a topic (44)

flashback..........a literary device that allows the narrator to tell readers about something that happened previously in the story or before the story (74)

homophone......words that sound the same but are spelled differently and mean different things (22)

inclusive language........language that is respectful and inclusive of diversity (57)

main idea..........the idea the writer or speaker wants you to believe or accept as true (44)

neologism..........a made-up word or when a new meaning is given to an existing word or a word borrowed from another language (51)

Grammar Rules! Student Book 4 (ISBN 9780655092520) © Tanya Gibb

noun..................a naming word for people, places, animals and things 8

to classify in a noun group 15 57 *noun group* 15

proper and common 8 *singular, plural and collective* 23

noun-verb agreement....a verb needs to agree with its subject in number 61

objective language........language that is factual and unbiased 56

plot.....................the events in a narrative 74

poetic language/imagery....words that help create a picture in the mind 16

possessive apostrophe....a punctuation mark used to show possession 25

prefix.................letters added to the beginning of words 16

prepositional phrase.....a group of words that consists of a preposition followed by a **noun** or **pronoun**; can tell time (when), place (where) or manner (how) 21

pronoun.............a word that refers to or replaces a noun 13

possessive pronoun 24

pun.....................usually humorous wordplay in which a word or phrase has more than one meaning 51

question.............a sentence that asks for information or an opinion; can be open or closed 28

quoted (direct) speech....the actual speech someone said 12

reference..........how **pronouns** (and **noun groups**) refer to one noun across a text 38

reported (indirect) speech....speech that is reported and not directly quoted 12

sentence...........a group of words that makes sense and includes at least one **verb** 11 15

complex 29 53 *simple and compound* 11 26

simile.................something is compared to something else using *like* or *as* 49

spoonerism.......when the beginning sounds of words are swapped 51

statement..........a sentence that gives information or an opinion 28

subjective language......shows a point of view, opinion or bias 56

suffix..................a letter or word part added to the end of a word

antonyms 16 *plurals* 23 *tense* 65

synonym...........when words have similar meanings 16

tense..................the way verbs anchor events in time 9 65

tension...............a feature of a narrative plot that keeps readers/viewers interested; conflict 74

verb....................a doing (action), relating (being), thinking, feeling, or saying word

doing (action) 9 *helping (auxiliary verb)* 40

modal verb 59 *relating (being)* 14

saying 9 12 *tense* 9 27 65

thinking 10 *verb group* 40 64

verb-subject agreement 61